36.95
SSA

REACHING THE HISPANIC MARKET EFFECTIVELY
The Media, the Market, the Methods

Antonio Guernica

with the collaboration of
Irene Kasperuk

McGraw-Hill Book Company

New York St. Louis San Francisco Auckland
Bogotá Hamburg Johannesburg London Madrid
Mexico Montreal New Delhi Panama Paris
São Paulo Singapore Sydney Tokyo Toronto

Library of Congress Cataloging in Publication Data

Guernica, Antonio.
    Reaching the Hispanic market effectively.

    Bibliography: p.
    Includes index.
    1. Hispanic Americans as consumers—United
States.   2. Marketing—United States.   I. Kasperuk,
Irene.   II. Title.
HC110.C6G83   658.8'04   81-20687
ISBN 0-07-025107-X   AACR2

1234567890   DODO   898765432

ISBN 0-07-025107-X

The editors for this book were William R. Newton and William
B. O'Neal, the designer was Mark E. Safran, and the production
supervisor was Sally Fliess. It was set in Gael by The Kingsport
Press.

Printed and bound by R. R. Donnelley & Sons Company.

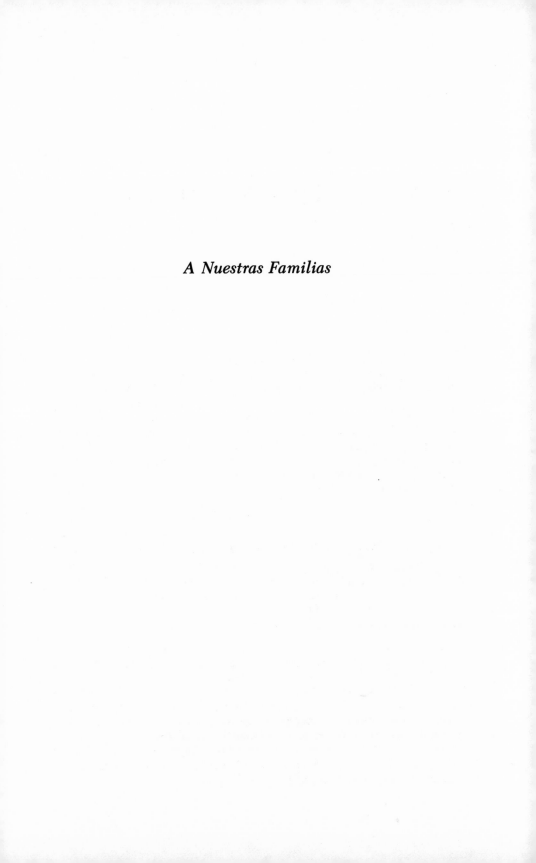

A Nuestras Familias

About the Authors

Antonio José Guernica

Guernica was born in Santiago de Cuba and came to the United States at the age of 10. He received his master's degree in radio-television-film from the University of Maryland. He has been executive vice president of the National Association of Spanish Broadcasters (NASB) since its inception and was one of the association's cofounders. As NASB vice president, Guernica coordinated and was editor of *U.S. Hispanics—A Market Profile,* the first national marketing study of the U.S. Hispanic population, published in 1980.

Before joining the NASB, Guernica held the position of research director for SIN–National Spanish Television Network. He also worked as staff writer for *Agenda* magazine, a national Hispanic journal. Guernica has also enjoyed success as an advertising and marketing consultant and as an independent producer.

He is currently completing editing work on a book on Hispanics and the mass media. Other publications by Guernica include numerous professional articles and papers on Hispanics and the mass media, marketing, and advertising.

Irene Kasperuk

Born in Caracas, Venezuela, Kasperuk came to the United States at the age of 11. She received her bachelor's degree in Spanish literature and Latin American area studies from Queens College.

While working in the editorial and advertising departments of Saral Publications in New York, Kasperuk gained considerable expertise in Spanish print media. Her experience in Spanish broadcasting comes from having worked in the research department of SIN–National Spanish Television Network.

Kasperuk has traveled extensively throughout Latin America and Europe and speaks five languages fluently. She is currently working as a marketing and advertising consultant and free-lance writer.

Contents

Preface   xi
Acknowledgments   xv
Semantic Notes   xvii

1. THE MEDIA. **1**

　1. Hispanics As a Target Audience   3

　2. Print.   9

　　Magazines   9
　　Newspapers   11
　　Conclusion   12
　　Listings—Spanish Print Media   13

　3. Radio—Listening Habits   17

　　Program Formats   19
　　Day-Parts   20
　　Audience Composition   21
　　Conclusion   22
　　Listings—Spanish-Format Radio Stations   23

　4. Television—Viewing Habits   35

　　Program Formats   39
　　Day-Parts   40
　　Audience Composition   41
　　Conclusion   42
　　Listings—Spanish-Format Television Stations   43

2. THE MARKET 47

5. Demographic Profile 49

World Rank   50
Age and Sex Distribution   50
Area of Origin   52
Population by Region and State   54
Hispanic Population Growth, 1970 to 1980   55
Hispanic Population Growth by Region, 1970 to 1980   56
Hispanic versus Total U.S. Population by Region   57
Hispanic versus Total U.S. Population by State   57
Household Size   59
Median Income by Spanish Origin   59
Median Income by Geographic Region   60
Education   61
Employment   64
Metropolitan versus Nonmetropolitan Residence   66
Top Thirty Hispanic Markets   67
United States–Mexico Border Markets   68
Conclusion   69

6. The Hispanic Presence 73

Mexico   74
Puerto Rico   78
Cuba   80
The Hispanic in American Society Today   82

7. Consumer Behavior 85

Consumption Indices   86

3. THE METHODS 101

8. Making the Decision 103

The Business Opportunity   106
Choosing the Agency   108
The Test Market   111
Conclusion   117
Listings—Hispanic Advertising Agencies   117

9. Creative Strategy 123

Language   124
Family Ties   126
The Catholic Religion   127
Attitudinal Similarities   128

Character Portrayal   130
Coordination with General Campaign   131
National versus Regional Approach   133
Additional Considerations   136
Conclusion   138

10. The Media Plan   141
Television   142
Radio   144
Print   146
Outdoor and Transit Advertising   147
Ratings   147
Reach and Frequency   152
Conclusion   154

11. Scott Paper Company—Case History   155

12. Trends and Projections.   163

Bibliography.   169

Index   183

Preface

In the last few years, the Hispanic population in the United States has been garnering an increasing amount of attention both from the media and from advertisers. Of note among the press coverage has been *Time* magazine's cover story "Hispanic Americans, Soon: The Biggest Minority," published in the October 16, 1978, issue. *Newsweek, U.S. News & World Report,* and numerous other national magazines closely followed or preceded the *Time* cover story with their own articles on the U.S. Hispanic population. Major newspapers such as *The New York Times* and *The Washington Post* have featured series of articles examining various aspects of the U.S. Hispanic population.

Advertising Age, Broadcasting, Adweek, Madison Avenue, Marketing & Media Decisions, and other broadcast and advertising trade magazines have devoted major articles to the U.S. Hispanic market. *Television/Radio Age* has featured a yearly Hispanic market issue since 1975. The dean of American broadcast journalism, Walter Cronkite, anchored a series of reports on the U.S. Hispanic population during 1980. More importantly, articles, news stories, and features on the U.S. Hispanic population, the Spanish media, and Hispanic advertising have increasingly become part of the regular media coverage.

To what mysterious force does the U.S. Hispanic market owe this newfound interest and recognition? The answer is hardly a mystery. Undeniably large growth has brought recognition to the U.S. Hispanic market—not market potential somewhere in the far-off future, but its current worth, right now.

In 1980, there were approximately 15 million Hispanics residing legally in the United States mainland, with an additional population of undocumented or illegal Hispanic aliens loosely estimated between

6 and 8 million. In 1980, the projected gross income for all U.S. Hispanics represented a market figure of over $70 billion.

From 1970 to 1980, the U.S. Hispanic population grew at a rate 6½ times that of the general population. Legal and illegal Hispanic immigration to the United States shows no sign of slackening, nor is immigration expected to decline appreciably until such time as Spanish-speaking countries, particularly Mexico, reach relative economic parity with the United States. Regional data indicate that Hispanic mothers are giving birth at a higher rate than the general population—giving birth to children whose first words will be in Spanish, whose attitudes and perceptions will be shaped initially within the Spanish-speaking environment of their homes.

Hispanic families are larger and younger than non-Hispanic families. The Hispanic population is largely urban and geographically concentrated and is therefore easy to reach through the appropriate mass media. Hispanics have demonstrated a capacity for upward mobility, and the median income of the Hispanic population should reflect this fact in the near future.

Demographic comparisons between the Hispanic and the general populations have drawn the attention of the media and of advertisers, but demographic characteristics only begin to define the U.S. Hispanic population as a distinct market. Beyond demographic characteristics U.S. Hispanics share in common certain cultural characteristics that are substantially different from those of the American mainstream. Moreover, these characteristics can be described and explained in operable terms that advertisers can utilize to optimally influence consumer behavior.

Cultural traits such as the use of the Spanish language, a strong Catholic tradition, close family ties, conservative moral and social values, and traditional personal roles characterize the lifestyle of the U.S. Hispanic. In tandem with the demographic characteristics of the U.S. Hispanic population, these cultural traits dictate the advertising message that will most effectively reach the market.

Spanish language media are an important part of the U.S. Hispanic lifestyle. The one trait that best defines the Hispanic market—use of the Spanish language—also characterizes the most effective way to reach it—through the Spanish language media. As the Hispanic population grows in size and importance, the Spanish media experience parallel growth as effective advertising vehicles.

This book provides an in-depth view of the Spanish media, accompanied by a close look at the U.S. Hispanic market, culminating in a comprehensive discussion of the methods used to reach it successfully through advertising.

The first part of the book, The Media, provides an overview of

Hispanics as a target audience and examines the individual appeals of Spanish print, radio, and television.

The second part, The Market, provides a strong conceptual framework of the Hispanic population as a market, featuring an extensive demographic profile of the population as well as its consumer behavior.

The final part, The Methods, offers the advertiser specific guidelines and recommendations for an effective advertising campaign geared toward U.S. Hispanics. It takes the advertiser from making the decision to enter the market through the planning stages, the creative strategy, and the media plan. By way of illustration, we take a comprehensive look at the Scott Paper Company's experiences in the Hispanic market.

The concluding chapter, Trends and Projections, looks toward the future of the U.S. Hispanic population and of the Spanish media and the changes that can be expected in Hispanic advertising.

We hope and believe that the information contained in this book will contribute to your success in reaching the U.S. Hispanic market today and in the future.

Antonio Guernica
Irene Kasperuk

Acknowledgments

There are many people who contributed toward making this book possible and to whom we would like to express our sincere appreciation. We extend our thanks to the people who made the time to share their experiences in the Hispanic market with us through interviews and conversations—Mr. Rene Anselmo, president, SIN–National Spanish Television Network; Mr. Carlos Barba, president, WNJU-TV Broadcasting Corporation; Mr. Eduardo Caballero, president, Caballero Spanish Media; Ms. Alicia Conill, executive vice president, Conill Advertising; Mr. Luis Diaz-Albertini, president, SAMS, Inc.; Dr. Marcelino Miyares, president, OMAR, Inc.; Mr. James Murtagh, business manager, the Bravo Group/Young & Rubicam, Inc.; Ms. Teresa Zubizarreta, president, Zubi Advertising. In this respect, we would especially like to recognize Mr. Richard Dillon, president, Mendoza, Dillon y Asociados, for his contribution to Chapter 8, Making the Decision, for his valuable insights, and for providing the case histories featured in the chapter.

This book owes much to five institutions in particular. Strategy Research Corporation (SRC) provided the bulk of the demographic data featured in Chapter 5, Demographic Profile, and the product consumption indices in Chapter 7, Consumer Behavior. Hispanic-audience television ratings generated by SRC were also essential in the writing of Chapter 4, Television—Viewing Habits. We extend our appreciation to Mr. Richard Tobin, president, and Mr. Peter Roslow, vice president, of SRC.

We would also like to thank The Arbitron Company and The Gallup Organization for their authorization to use their audience data and reports.

We wish to express our gratitude to Mr. Malcolm Douglas Gray, director of advertising services, and to the Scott Paper Company as a whole, for granting us permission to use Scott's Hispanic market experience as a case history.

We are indebted to the National Association of Spanish Broadcasters (NASB) for providing the lists of Spanish-format radio and television stations that appear in Chapter 3, Radio—Listening Habits, and Chapter 4, Television—Viewing Habits. Our warm appreciation goes to Ms. Carmen Junco, president of NASB, for her support while the book was in progress.

Ms. Carol McDougall's enthusiastic contribution in preparing the manuscript was invaluable and is deeply appreciated by the authors.

Without the active participation of these people, this book would not have become a reality. Thank you.

Semantic Notes

"Hispanics," "Spanish-speaking," "Spanish-surnamed," "Spanish origin," "Latino"—these terms all have been widely used to refer to that population segment in the United States whose members originally came from a Spanish-speaking country. Often the terms have been used interchangeably, without regard for definition, allowing each to derive its meaning (or, rather, its lack of meaning) from popular use. Demographic and cultural characteristics belonging to one population segment have occasionally been attributed to another out of convenience or self-interest.

While there is a substantial degree of overlapping among these various groups in number and characteristics, they are not identical.

In this text, the word "Hispanic" will refer to that population segment with the capability of speaking and comprehending the Spanish language, whose ancestry is based on a Spanish-speaking country, and which identifies with the Hispanic culture. Any divergence from this definition when attributed to a population segment will be noted in the text.

"Spanish-speaking" refers to that population with the ability to speak and comprehend the Spanish language, whether as a primary or secondary language. This term may encompass non-Hispanics as well as Hispanics.

"Spanish-surnamed" refers to the population segment whose last name has been identified as Spanish by the U.S. Census Bureau. "Spanish-surnamed" does not include Hispanics with non-Spanish last names and does include non-Hispanics whose last names are Spanish. These situations are most commonly associated with marriage and the adoption of the husband's name.

"Spanish origin" refers to that segment of the population who came from a Spanish-speaking country or whose ancestors came from a Spanish-speaking country. The term "Spanish origin" does not necessarily indicate that the person is Spanish-speaking or personally identifies with the Hispanic culture.

"Latino" or "Latin" refers to people whose language is based on Latin, the language of the ancient Romans. The term "Latino" includes people using the French, Italian, Portuguese, or Spanish languages.

THE MEDIA

PART

1

Chapter 1

Hispanics As a Target Audience

The communications media in this country have traditionally sought the largest and widest audience possible. In this pursuit the mass media have chosen, as a matter of policy, the path of least offensiveness in their content. The philosophy of programmers and editors has not been to provide content that strongly appeals, that elicits a forceful response from the audience, but rather to present neutral media content.

The rationale behind this policy is pretty straightforward. Media content that strongly attracts a certain segment of the audience, generally, will strongly repel another segment of the audience. The mass media do not require intensity to be financially successful; they demand numbers, the larger the better.

Newspapers and magazines price their advertising space according to circulation. Radio and television base their rate cards on the size of the audience they reach. Advertisers are interested in exposing their products to as many people as they can.

This philosophy of neutral media content made particularly good business sense when the public had access to relatively few mass media outlets. As the number of media outlets increased, a gradual shift in policy toward increased targeting of media content developed.

This targeting is particularly evident among magazines in the print media and among radio in the broadcast media. As the circulations of *Life* and *Look* declined, magazines such as *Sports Illustrated* thrived. Magazine content narrowed even further, focusing on specific interests, as indicated by the emergence of such magazines as

Road and Track, Popular Photography, and *Skiing.* Lifestyle magazines such as *Cosmopolitan, Playboy,* and *Ebony* joined a trend that has not yet reached its peak. As the focus of magazine content narrowed, advertisers became increasingly concerned with the type, as well as the size, of the audience the magazine was reaching.

Newspapers retained their cross-sectional appeal but increasingly organized their formats into sections devoted to specific interests. Sections were added to attract readers who would not regularly buy the paper merely for the basic news coverage. The emergence of special-interest columns and features began to play a greater part in readership promotion efforts. Elements as unrelated to basic news coverage as comic strips became promotional tools. When the comic strip *Doonesbury* went from *The Washington Post* to *The Washington Star,* the *Star* developed an extensive promotional campaign around its new acquisition, complete with television spots, posters, and bumper stickers.

Media segmentation has become increasingly evident in broadcasting. Essentially a segmented medium since television became dominant, radio, of necessity, quickly recognized the positive side of directing programming at a specific audience segment. A growing variety of formats with narrow target audiences—top forty, country and western, classical, all-news, middle-of-the-road, album rock, black, beautiful music, disco—all have made a place for themselves.

Since the radio audience "pie" is only so big, competition for the same audience among the different formats, and particularly among stations with similar formats, naturally continued. But each radio station planned its programming content with one particular listener profile in mind.

With the exception of foreign language programming, television has remained the most purely mass appeal medium. Admittedly, there is a diversity of program fare on television appealing to distinct audience segments—NFL football does not have the same appeal as *Charlie's Angels.* Nevertheless, both are watched by many of the same people. The boundaries of profitable audience segmentation are severely limited.

These boundaries are particularly limited when it comes to network entertainment programming, which makes up the bulk of prime-time fare. The Monday through Friday, 8:00 to 11:00 P.M. time period guarantees each of the three networks an audience of millions, only slightly affected by the programming they offer. The networks do not have to entice the audience of millions to turn on the television set. Prime time has its own momentum. Millions of television sets are already turned on, overwhelmingly to the network stations. It is then not so much a matter of giving the viewer a reason to turn on a particular channel as it is a matter of preventing the viewer from switching to a competing station. Given this ready audience of millions, the networks design the program content to be the least objectionable to the largest number of people.

Since the independent television stations operate at the local level rather than at the national network level, they can focus on local programming desires or on the desires of a section of the local audience. For example, the independents provide coverage of local sports, both professional and college, which may not have sufficient national appeal to be carried by the networks. Just as radio stations position their programming so as to attract a specific audience segment, independent television stations try to offer a type of programming which the networks are not offering at that particular time period.

In an environment of positioning media content and audience segmentation, the emergence of Hispanic-oriented media is a logical and predictable occurrence. The development of Hispanic-oriented media actually remained dormant for too long because the people involved in the media industry were unfamiliar with the audience. As it became evident that targeting content to Hispanics would produce profits, Hispanic-oriented media began to develop. In the last 10 years, this development has been spurred by an unprecedented emphasis on ethnic and cultural identity.

As a target audience, Hispanics are well-defined and accessible. U.S. Hispanics are geographically concentrated; they can therefore be effectively reached through the use of a minimum number of media outlets. The three major Hispanic groups—Mexicans, Puerto Ricans, and Cubans—are geographically separated, thereby facilitating the tailoring of local and regional media to each group.

U.S. Hispanics are most receptive to media content in the Spanish language. Spanish programming elicits an emotional response from the Hispanic audience that is missing in English language media. Throughout the history of U.S. Hispanics, their ties to Hispanic language and culture have been demonstrably enduring.

Virtually all U.S. Hispanic-oriented media are in the Spanish language, although rare exceptions exist in magazines and noncommercial television programming. Similarly, most Hispanic-oriented media content has been imported from the countries of origin of the U.S. Hispanic population, with Mexico providing the bulk at the national level.

Hispanic-oriented media in the United States function as a bridge between U.S. Hispanics and their countries of origin. Magazines generally cover personalities and events in the Hispanic world that have their greatest impact and importance outside of the United States. It is an exception when a Spanish radio station plays the song of a

U.S.-based Hispanic artist. Although national news is covered, radio stations emphasize news coverage of events taking place in their audiences' countries of origin, as well as local Hispanic news. U.S. Spanish language television stations usually produce their own local news and public affairs programs, a rare series, and an occasional special within the United States, but these are exceptions to the rule.

Because of their reliance on foreign imports and use of the Spanish language, the heaviest consumers of Hispanic-oriented media in this country consist of recent Hispanic immigrants to the United States and of Hispanics with limited English speaking ability. While this audience is generally a low-income audience, it represents literally tens of billions of dollars in disposable income yearly. It also represents a proportionately heavier buying market of food and selected products than does the general population.

This core audience is the heaviest consumer of Hispanic media content because it does not have other viable alternatives. Spanish monolingual Hispanics cannot understand English media. They are in effect limited to choosing among the available Spanish media, which are few in comparison with the general-audience media.

This core audience devotes most of its media-consuming time to very few Hispanic outlets. Monolingual Hispanics listen to their favorite Spanish radio station and view their favorite Spanish television station with greater frequency and for longer periods of time than their general-audience counterparts spend listening to their favorite radio or watching their favorite television station. Monolingual Hispanics purchase their favorite magazines with greater regularity and read them more thoroughly than do their general-audience counterparts. It is all a matter of what is realistically available to satiate the appetite for media consumption.

The secondary audience for Hispanic-oriented media is made up of bilingual Hispanics. Although secondary in terms of the degree of Hispanic media consumption, this audience is the largest and most important segment of Hispanic media's total audience. According to the U.S. Bureau of the Census, 76 percent of the U.S. Spanish-origin population is bilingual.

There are some striking differences between this audience segment and the core audience. Whereas the core audience has limited media choices in comparison with the general audience, the bilingual Hispanic can choose from both general and Hispanic-oriented media. The bilingual Hispanic's economic standing and disposable income are near that of the general population, although buying habits differ. The bilingual Hispanic may very well work in an English-speaking environment but speak Spanish at home. Bilingual Hispanics participate in American society without assimilating. Their cultural values differ from those of the general population.

The bilingual Hispanic is attracted to Hispanic media by the combination of language and cultural orientation. Hispanic cultural values are not as a rule reflected in general-audience media content. Hispanic media content comes much closer to presenting a view of the world as seen through the eyes of the bilingual Hispanic. Again, there is an emotional response to Hispanic media that is usually missing in the case of general-audience media.

This does not mean that bilingual Hispanics do not use English language media. Indeed they do; they just do not use general-audience media anywhere near as frequently or for the same duration as the population at large does. If the bilingual Hispanic's use of Hispanic media were factored out, his or her complete media-habit profile would look surprisingly similar to that of the general population, at least as it relates to broadcast choices. Radio formats and television programs that are most popular with the general audience would tend to hold the same position with bilingual Hispanic viewers and listeners—if their options were restricted to general-audience media. In most instances, however, the bilingual Hispanic does have Hispanic-oriented media available and often chooses to use them.

There is also a marginal and occasional audience of Hispanic media consisting of Hispanics and non-Hispanics with limited Spanish speaking ability. They may be able to understand Spanish but not necessarily to speak it, for instance.

This marginal audience closely approximates the general audience in its media habits and should be considered as a bonus by Spanish media advertisers. Hispanic media formats that draw this third audience can be characterized as having content that requires limited comprehension of the Spanish language in order to be enjoyed. Principal among these formats are bilingual magazines, Hispanic music on Spanish radio, and sports and variety programs on Spanish television. The cultural attraction aspect of Hispanic media has slight relevance to this audience.

The two main ingredients that characterize Hispanic media are use of the Spanish language and presentation of Hispanic cultural values. The incidence of Hispanic-media use in a particular area will be in direct proportion to the degree that these traits are found in the potential audience. Given an audience capable of financially supporting competing Hispanic broadcast media, the radio or television station that most effectively targets its programming to the cultural subtleties of the Hispanic population in its coverage area will certainly draw the largest and most faithful Hispanic audience.

Chapter 2

Print

In comparison with the numerous magazines, weeklies, and dailies available to the general market in the United States, there is a relatively small quantity of print content aimed at U.S. Hispanics. As an advertising medium for reaching Hispanics, print comes in a poor second to broadcasting. As a group, U.S. Hispanics tend to be light readers, turning instead toward the more popular media of Spanish radio and television for most information and entertainment needs.

Once a Spanish magazine is in the hands of a Hispanic reader, however, it is thoroughly read and it enjoys a high pass-along readership rate. Spanish print, like Spanish broadcast media, provides an emotional and informational tie to the Hispanic culture, often to a specific country of origin. The editorial content of Spanish print, be it fictional or factual, is culturally in tune with the Hispanic reader.

MAGAZINES

Approximately twenty-five Spanish language magazines enjoy national distribution in the United States today. The most successful Spanish magazines have been traditionally geared toward the Hispanic woman. *Vanidades* entered the U.S. market in 1961, making it the first Spanish women's magazine available nationally. Since then the number of national Spanish publications has gradually grown and diversified, although Spanish women's magazines have retained their prominence in the marketplace.

Hispanics can now choose among a wide variety of magazines catering to individual needs and interests. *Hombre de Mundo*'s editorial content concentrates on topics which appeal to the sophisticated "man of the world." *Cosmopolitan en Español* is written for the young, modern, self-oriented Latin woman. Boxing fans can appreciate the in-depth coverage of the latest boxing bouts and world boxing championships when they read *The Ring en Español*. *Coqueta* provides the younger *latina* with youth-oriented articles to serve her interests and is written in her vernacular.

In the past decade, Hispanic women's magazines such as *Vanidades, Buenhogar,* and *Cosmopolitan en Español* have particularly experienced tremendous popularity with U.S. Hispanic women. Each of these publications is aimed at a different target group within the Hispanic women segment—*Vanidades* aims at women 18 to 49 years old, *Buenhogar* pursues the young housewife between 18 and 34 years of age, and *Cosmopolitan* goes after the upscale career woman. Yet there are common threads in the editorial content of these three magazines, as in all Hispanic women's magazines.

This editorial content is very much in line with conservative Hispanic cultural values, stressing the importance of harmony within the family and emphasizing the Hispanic woman's traditional role as wife, mother, and homemaker. Magazines such as *Cosmopolitan* and *Coqueta* do exercise some flexibility within these boundaries. The basic editorial content of Hispanic women's magazines covers fashion, beauty, decoration, male-female relationships, food, entertainment, personalities, and light fiction.

Hispanic women's magazines generally enjoy a high rate of pass-along readership, each copy being read by over four readers. Pass-along readership is particularly high among the more-established magazines. Hispanic women's magazines are thoroughly read and are not discarded lightly. Ideas for decorating, fashion, and recipes carried in the magazines are all extensively used. Advertising offering similar tips is also appreciated. It is common for the Hispanic woman to keep a particular issue around the house for months, simply because it contains one of her favorite recipes or decorating hints.

In addition to magazines with national distribution, there are a number of Spanish magazines which enjoy success at the local and regional levels. Magazines in Miami catering to the well-educated Hispanic population do particularly well.

Since the editorial content of Hispanic magazines stresses Hispanic cultural values and emphasizes coverage of events and personalities outside of the United States, it is natural that most Hispanic magazines are in the Spanish language. Use of the Spanish language reinforces the emotional ties to culture and country of origin that most Hispanic magazines provide.

There are some notable exceptions, however, such as *Nuestro* magazine. Ninety to one hundred percent of the editorial content in

Nuestro is in English and concentrates on people and events within the United States. While the language of the magazine is English, the editorial emphasis is definitely on topics of special interest to Hispanics. This choice of English language editorial content is based on the fact that according to the U.S. Census Bureau, 76 percent of U.S. Hispanics are bilingual.

Upon making its entry into the Hispanic market as a national magazine, *Nuestro* estimated that over 1 million U.S. Hispanic families were potential readers of a Spanish magazine printed in English. From the outset, *Nuestro* encountered problems in distribution, developing its circulation, and increasing its subscribers. Advertising was very slow in coming. In the three critical areas of advertising, circulation, and distribution, *Nuestro* fell short of expectations.

Strong retention of the Spanish language has been one of the most distinguishable and enduring traits among U.S. Hispanics. Spanish language magazines are doing much better as a whole than English language Hispanic magazines, most likely because the emotional tie to the Hispanic culture provided by Spanish language editoral content is usually missing when the magazine uses the English language.

NEWSPAPERS

There are eight Spanish language newspapers in the United States published daily, among them, *La Opinión* in Los Angeles, *Diario Las Américas* and *El Miami Herald* in Miami, and *El Diario–La Prensa* in New York, published every day but Saturday.

Spanish newspapers reflect the Hispanic composition of their readership in their news coverage. The Los Angeles papers, with a primarily Mexican-origin readership, emphasize coverage of Mexican-American personalities and events, features on specifically Mexican-interest topics, and news of Mexico itself, particularly U.S.-Mexican relations. In addition to covering the local Cuban community, the two Miami newspapers are deeply concerned with U.S.-Cuban relations. The character of the primarily Cuban-refugee Hispanic population of Miami is strongly reflected in the editorials of the two papers.

El Diario–La Prensa emphasizes coverage of news from Puerto Rico without neglecting the news from Central and South American countries that is of interest to the other important segments of the New York Hispanic population. *El Diario–La Prensa*'s involvement in the local Hispanic community is reflected in both its news coverage and its editorial policy.

All these Spanish newspapers are effective advocates for the Hispanic community, taking strong editorial positions as a matter of course on issues that concern their readership. These newspapers represent an important source for timely, in-depth information about events of particular interest to Hispanics, news that would not be covered by a general-audience newspaper.

In addition to the daily newspapers, there are numerous Spanish weeklies and biweeklies published in cities such as Chicago, San Francisco, and San Antonio, as well as in cities with smaller but concentrated Hispanic populations. The weeklies generally have a smaller circulation than the dailies. The weeklies emphasize news of local interest to a greater degree than the daily newspapers do, providing comprehensive coverage of community affairs and upcoming events of local Hispanic organizations and groups. For the weeklies, involvement in the local Hispanic community is the salient priority. Columns with the distinctive style of a local and respected reporter, very active editorial policy, and strong Hispanic advocacy characterize the Hispanic weekly.

CONCLUSION

National Spanish magazines generally concentrate on providing editorial content on personalities, events, and features that have their greatest impact outside of the United States. Within the boundaries of traditional Hispanic cultural values, each magazine tailors its editorial content to attract a specific audience segment, primarily the Hispanic woman.

While Spanish magazines emphasize themes from outside the United States, Spanish newspapers face the task of complementing their strong international coverage of Hispanic countries with active reporting of local news and events of particular interest to Hispanics. Spanish newspapers need to be deeply involved in the Hispanic community to be most successful. Lead articles on local Hispanic personalities and events share the front page of Spanish newspapers with international news from Hispanic countries. U.S. national news is usually considered of lesser priority to the Spanish newspaper's readership and is relegated to smaller headlines or to the back pages.

Newspaper advertising rates are usually low. As a complementary advertising medium to broadcasting, Spanish newspapers are extremely credible and an excellent vehicle for communicating technical or factual information and concepts that cannot be easily imparted through the broadcast media.

Products that are used on a regular basis by women should do especially well when advertised in Spanish magazines. Offering new practical and creative uses for the product is a particularly effective advertising strategy.

Hispanic print can in general be used very effectively to support and complement a Hispanic advertising campaign centered around the Spanish broadcast media.

LISTINGS—SPANISH PRINT MEDIA

Spanish Magazines

The following list is alphabetical by title of publication. These magazines are distributed nationally in high-Hispanic-population centers.

Key to Listings:

First line	Title	Telephone
Second line	Publisher	
Third line	Address	
Fourth line	Language of text, frequency of publication, primary readership	

Agenda   (202) 293-4680
National Council of La Raza
1725 I St., N.W., Washington, DC 20006
Bilingual, bimonthly, organizations—professional and community

Buenhogar   (212) 687-8760
De Armas Publications
605 Third Ave., New York, NY 10016
Spanish, semimonthly, women 18–54

Caminos   (714) 889-0539
Caminos Corporation
107 E. 6th St., San Bernardino, CA 92410
Bilingual, Monthly

Coqueta   (212) 687-8760
De Armas Publications
605 Third Ave., New York, NY 10016
Spanish, fortnightly, women 15–25

Cosmopolitan en Español   (212) 687-8760
De Armas Publications
605 Third Ave., New York, NY 10016
Spanish, monthly, women 18–39

Fascinación   (212) 687-8760
De Armas Publications
605 Third Ave., New York, NY 10016
Spanish, monthly, women 18–34

Geomundo   (212) 687-8760
De Armas Publications
605 Third Ave., New York, NY 10016
Spanish, monthly, family

Gráfica   (213) 462-2481
Orbe Publications
705 N. Windsor Blvd., Hollywood, CA 90029
Spanish, bimonthly, family

Harper's Bazaar en Español   (212) 687-8760
De Armas Publications
605 Third Ave., New York, NY 10016
Spanish, monthly, women 25–39

Hispanic Business   (805) 964-9041
Hispanic Business Publications
4672 Via Huerto, Santa Barbara, CA 93110
English, monthly, professionals

Hombre de Mundo   (212) 687-8760
De Armas Publications
605 Third Ave., New York, NY 10016
Spanish, monthly, men 18+

Ideas   (212) 687-8760
De Armas Publications
605 Third Ave., New York, NY 10016
Spanish, monthly, women 18–49

Intimidades   (212) 687-8760
De Armas Publications
605 Third Ave., New York, NY 10016
Spanish, bimonthly, men/women 18+

La Luz   (303) 831-4341
La Luz Publications Co., Inc.
1000 Logan St., Denver, CO 80203
English, monthly (except July and August), men/women 18+

Mecánica Popular   (212) 687-8760
De Armas Publications
605 Third Ave., New York, NY 10016
Spanish, monthly, men 18+

Nuestro   (212) 684-5999
Nuestro Publications, Inc.
461 Park Ave. South
Bilingual (90% English), monthly, men/women 18+

(Selecciones del) Reader's Digest   (212) 972-4000
Reader's Digest Association
200 Park Ave., New York, NY 10166
Spanish, monthly, men/women 18+

El Ring en Español   (212) 687-8760
De Armas Publications
605 Third Ave., New York, NY 10016
Spanish, monthly, men 18+

Temas   (212) 582-4750
Temas Magazine Corporation
1650 Broadway, New York, NY 10019
Spanish, monthly, family

Vanidades   (212) 687-8760
De Armas Publications
605 Third Ave., New York, NY 10016
Spanish, biweekly, women 18+

Spanish Newspapers

The following list is alphabetical by state and city. Circulation size
is as of January 1981. The newspapers are dailies and in the Spanish
language except as noted.

Key to Listings:

First line	Title	Telephone
Second line	Address	
Third line	Circulation	

CALIFORNIA

Los Angeles

La Opinión   (213) 748-2141
1436 S. Main St., Los Angeles, CA 90015
42,000

FLORIDA

Miami

Diario de las Américas   (305) 633-3341
2900 N.W. 39th St., Miami, FL 33142
55,000

El Miami Herald   (305) 350-2111
Old Herald Plaza, Miami, FL 33101
56,000

NEW YORK

New York

El Diario–La Prensa   (212) 553-0600
181 Hudson St., New York, NY 10013
65,000 (except Saturday)

Noticias de Este Mundo   (212) 684-5656
401 Fifth Ave., New York, NY 10016
10,000

TEXAS

Brownsville

The Brownsville Herald   (512) 542-4301
P.O. Box 351, Brownsville, TX 78520
16,500 (Spanish-English)

El Paso

El Continental   (915) 532-6587
2300 E. Yandell, El Paso, TX 79003
4000

Laredo

Laredo Times   (512) 723-2901
P.O. Box 2129, Laredo, TX 78041
20,000 (Spanish-English)

Chapter 3

Radio –
Listening Habits

In the United States an estimated 150 radio stations broadcast Spanish language programming from 10 hours a week to full-time. Approximately 100 of these stations broadcast full-time in Spanish. Although these are located primarily in Texas, California, and the southwestern states, there are clusters of stations in New York City, Chicago, Miami, and other pockets of high Hispanic concentration.

These Spanish language stations compete among themselves and, to a lesser degree, with English language media for the Hispanic listener. As a format, Spanish language programming is doing quite well in attracting the Hispanic audience, consistently delivering audience shares of over 40 percent, Monday through Sunday, 6:00 A.M. to midnight among Hispanics 12 years old and over. In cities such as Miami, San Antonio, and El Paso, Spanish-format stations hold the number 1 or 2 position in the market among all radio stations.

Spanish radio communicates person-to-person; its appeal is to the individual. Spanish radio acts as a culturally attuned companion to its listeners. Radio tells Hispanics that they are not alone in a society with values that are notably different from those of a traditionally Hispanic society. Similarly, the radio's familiar music and language tend to reassure Hispanics that they belong, that they do have a place in American society. And since the radio does not demand total attention, the listener can cook, drive a car, work, or take care of the kids with the radio as a constant adult companion.

Spanish radio is an informed and credible companion. Spanish stations serve as the primary source of news and information for many of the Spanish-speaking people in their coverage area. News from the country of origin is particularly appreciated. The U.S. Hispanic strives to keep ties to the homeland alive. The news carried by the Spanish station about its audience's country of origin provides an informational tie to the homeland.

Music, which constitutes the bulk of Spanish radio's programming, plays a different role in the ties to the Hispanic culture. The music serves a cultural mood-setting function by providing a musical atmosphere or background similar to that of the country of origin. The music provides a more purely emotional bond to the Hispanic culture.

Spanish radio's combination of informational and emotional ties to the country of origin forms an appeal that is stronger than the sum of its parts. This is particularly true because both elements are reinforced by their presence within a Spanish language framework. Spanish radio creates a programming environment in which Hispanics are comfortable. It creates programming that is emotionally rewarding, credible, and relevant to them. In essence, Spanish radio represents a direct electrical connection to the Hispanic culture and language.

Community involvement is an added factor that greatly contributes to Spanish radio's popularity. Strong community involvement is particularly evident among the most successful stations.

Spanish radio has the ability to focus in on the local Hispanic community and identify itself with the community's interests through its programming. The type of Hispanic music the station plays reflects the composition of the local Hispanic audience. In a market such as San Francisco, with a substantial South American population in addition to its sophisticated Mexican population, the playlist reflects music that is popular in a cosmopolitan center such as Mexico City. Stations operating closer to the border tend to play more *musica norteña*, the country and western-like music of northern Mexico, and "Tex-Mex" music. Stations on the east coast program Caribbean music and salsa, adjusting their playlists to the audience's taste largely according to country of origin.

Although music is the primary element in radio programming, most stations also carry news, *novelas* or soap operas, public affairs programs, and community calendars. With the exception of *novelas,* most elements in the station's programming reflect community involvement.

The newscasts concentrate on events of interest to the local Hispanic community and on news events in the country of origin; U.S. national news is of lesser priority. Public affairs programs deal with Hispanic issues of local interest that are not necessarily of interest to the local non-Hispanic population or to Hispanic communities in other cities. Community calendars cover events and topics such as local celebrations of Hispanic holidays, job listings, meetings and events of local Hispanic organizations or neighborhood groups, charitable drives in the Hispanic community, and social services information.

Spanish radio's deep involvement in the community can be seen in its ability to mobilize its listeners. If a listener calls in saying that a small child is lost and asks for help, within moments of the station's broadcasting a description of the child and where he or she was last seen, numbers of listeners will likely go out in search of the youngster. If a family finds itself without home or food because of a fire or flood, the station appeals to its listeners and can expect money quickly to start coming in. Appeals for donations to aid the victims of natural disasters in Hispanic countries are quickly organized by the radio stations, and the response is usually fast and generous.

Strong community involvement is not only due to the Spanish radio station's operations; it is also a function of the community it serves. Because of its limited assimilation into the overall community, the Hispanic population is perceived by others and itself as a community complete in itself. Spanish radio stations are perceived as voices of the Hispanic community. The radio stations speak for the community. This greatly differs from the way general-audience stations are perceived, even by their most avid listeners.

PROGRAM FORMATS

The Spanish language format is the number 1 radio format among Hispanics, followed by the contemporary format. Spanish-format radio stations generally capture over 40 percent of the audience share among Hispanics 12 years of age and older in their coverage area according to Arbitron reports.

In 1978, The Arbitron Company released the fourth report in its series *How Blacks and Spanish Listen to Radio.* This report covered Spanish listening habits in the metropolitan areas of El Paso, Los Angeles, Miami, New York, and San Antonio from October 1976 to May 1977. According to this report, the Spanish-format audience shares among Hispanics 12 years old and over from 6:00 A.M. to midnight, Monday through Sunday, were 33 percent for El Paso, 25 percent for Los Angeles, 70 percent for Miami, 41 percent for New York, and 41 percent for San Antonio. The Arbitron report also stated that Spanish-format stations and contemporary-format stations combine to produce an audience share of approximately 70 percent among Hispanics 12 and older, from 6:00 A.M. to midnight, Monday through Sunday. Other formats divide the remaining 30 percent of the Hispanic audience 12 and older. In descending order these formats are black, beautiful music, news/talk, middle-of-the-road, country, religious, and classical/jazz. An advertiser interested in reaching the Hispanic population through radio can effectively limit the choice of stations in the media plan.

In the non-Hispanic population 12 years old and older, audience shares by format are much more evenly distributed, with contemporary, news/talk, beautiful music, black, and middle-of-the-road formats each gathering significant shares. In order to reach a level of penetration in the non-Hispanic audience comparable with that in the Hispanic audience, the advertiser has to consider buying advertising time on a much larger number of stations.

DAY-PARTS[1]

Overall, Hispanics have higher listening levels than the non-Hispanic population for all four day-parts—morning drive time (6:00 to 10:00 A.M., Monday through Friday), midday (10:00 A.M. to 3:00 P.M., Monday through Friday), afternoon drive time (3:00 to 7:00 P.M., Monday through Friday), and nighttime (7:00 P.M. to midnight, Monday through Friday). For the time period 6:00 A.M. to midnight, Monday through Sunday, Hispanics produce higher average ratings than non-Hispanics for persons 12 years old and older. The cumulative rating total for Hispanics 12 and older during this time period is similar to that for non-Hispanics.

The difference between Hispanic and non-Hispanic listening levels is particularly pronounced during the midday day-part. For Hispanics 12 and older, the midday day-part is usually the first- or second-highest time period for Spanish listening levels. It usually produces average ratings comparable with the morning drive-time day-part and significantly higher than the afternoon drive-time day-part.

This pattern differs greatly from that of the non-Hispanic population, where listening levels fall off dramatically after the morning drive-time day-part. If the advertiser is looking for a large number of Hispanic listeners at inexpensive rates, the 10:00 A.M. to 3:00 P.M., Monday through Friday day-part may represent a very efficient buy.

---

[1] Much of the data on Hispanic listening habits according to day-parts was drawn from The Arbitron Company, *How Blacks and Spanish Listen to Radio*, Reports 1–4, 1975, 1978; The Arbitron Company, *Measuring the Hispanic Radio Audience—A Report on the Hispanic Ethnic Procedures Study from Arbitron Research*, September 1979; Peter Roslow, "An Analysis of Spanish Radio Use" (unpublished master's thesis, New York University), 1976.

The nighttime day-part is the lightest Hispanic listening period by far, usually delivering approximately half of the audience delivered by the other day-parts. The nighttime day-part does provide higher average ratings among Hispanics 12 and older than it does among non-Hispanics.

AUDIENCE COMPOSITION

An overview of the demographic profile of the Hispanic radio audience would reveal two major findings according to age and sex: (1) more Hispanic women than men listen to Spanish-format stations and for longer periods of time, and (2) Hispanics 35 years of age and older display greater preference for Spanish-format stations than do younger Hispanics, although Hispanics 18 and older also demonstrate a strong preference.

Hispanics 12 and older spend over 40 percent of their listening time with a Spanish-format station. Low-income Hispanics listen to Spanish-format stations to a greater degree than do more affluent Hispanics. Among the various Hispanic groups, Cubans demonstrate a stronger preference for Spanish-format stations than do Puerto Ricans or Mexicans.

These were the general findings from a national telephone survey conducted from June 8 to July 6, 1979, by the Gallup Organization of 1015 respondents of Hispanic descent in Spanish-surname households listed in the phone book. The survey, *Listening and Viewing Habits of Hispanic Americans,* was released by Gallup in September 1979.

Men 18 Years of Age and Older   According to Arbitron reports on Hispanic listening habits, the first choice of radio formats among Hispanic men 18 years old and older is Spanish, with contemporary-format stations as a strong second. The morning drive-time day-part delivers the highest number of Hispanic men in this age group, followed by the midday and the afternoon drive-time day-parts in closely descending order. The nighttime day-part produces less than half of the audience delivered by any of the three other day-parts.

According to the Gallup Organization survey, 63 percent of Hispanic men listen to a Spanish-format radio station each weekday. The amount of time Hispanic men reported that they spent listening to Spanish radio each weekday was as follows: up to 1 hour, 25 percent; between 1 and 3 hours, 20 percent; between 3 and 5 hours, 8 percent; and 5 hours or more, 6 percent.

Women 18 Years of Age and Older   Arbitron radio reports indicate that Hispanic women 18 years old and older spend approximately 50 percent of their radio listening time with Spanish-format stations, preferring Spanish formats by a 2 to 1 margin over contemporary formats. Both the morning drive-time and the midday day-parts deliver high ratings for Hispanic women. There is a sharp drop in the Hispanic women audience during the afternoon drive-time day-part. The nighttime day-part generally delivers less than a third of the Hispanic women audience than does the midday or the morning drive-time day-part.

The Gallup survey reports that 61 percent of Hispanic women listen to Spanish radio each weekday: 15 percent listen from ½ to 1 hour, 20 percent usually listen from 1 to 3 hours, 13 percent listen from 3 to 5 hours, and 10 percent listen for 5 or more hours per weekday.

Teenagers (Ages 12 to 17)   Hispanic teenagers show a strong preference for contemporary-format stations, distantly followed by black-format stations, according to Arbitron. Spanish radio represents the third choice for Hispanic teenagers. On the whole, Hispanic teenagers spend less time listening to the radio than do older Hispanics. However, they do spend more time with radio during the afternoon drive-time day-part and are also more likely to be listening to the radio during the nighttime day-part than are older Hispanics.

Age Comparison   According to the Gallup study, 58 percent of Hispanics between 18 and 34 years of age listen to Spanish radio each weekday. Listening time breaks down as follows: 17 percent up to 1 hour, 19 percent 1 to 3 hours, 12 percent 3 to 5 hours, and 6 percent 5 hours or more.

Approximately 65 percent of Hispanics 35 to 49 years old spend time each weekday listening to Spanish stations: 22 percent listen up to 1 hour, 19 percent listen between 1 and 3 hours, 11 percent listen between 3 and 5 hours, and 10 percent listen for 5 or more hours each weekday.

Of Hispanics 50 years or older, 65 percent listen to a Spanish radio station every weekday: up to 1 hour, 24 percent; 1 to 3 hours, 18 percent; 3 to 5 hours, 10 percent; and 5 hours or more, 8 percent.

CONCLUSION

The strong identification of the Hispanic community with Spanish radio contributes greatly to the effectiveness of the advertising carried by the stations. The comfortable programming environment, the built-in credibility, and the emotional ties to the language and culture provided by the station all extend, by association, to the station's advertisements. Additionally, the listeners recognize that the company advertising in Spanish on their station has a special interest in presenting the product to *them* specifically. The listeners respond to the advertising as they respond to the programming.

The Hispanic audience spends more time listening to the radio than does the general audience. Hispanics spend the large majority of their listening time with Spanish-format stations first and contemporary-format stations second. The audience for Spanish-format radio stations is generally very loyal to its favorite station, resulting in low audience turnover and low crossover among Spanish-format stations. The advertiser can usually reach a significant portion of the local Hispanic market by buying advertising time on two or three radio stations only, a situation which facilitates the buying as well as the monitoring of advertising.

Essentially, Spanish radio offers a credible medium which delivers maximum coverage of a loyal and well-defined audience to the advertiser willing to make a limited investment.

LISTINGS—SPANISH-FORMAT RADIO STATIONS[2]

The following list is alphabetical by state and city of license. "Spanish-format radio stations" are defined as stations that broadcast for 50 percent or more of their air time in the Spanish language. Most of the stations in the listings are full-time Spanish language radio stations.

Key to Listings:

First line   Call letters Frequency in kHz or MHz Telephone
Second line   Address
Third line   General manager

ARIZONA

Phoenix
KIFN-AM   860 kHz   (602) 257-9363
147 E. Garfield, Phoenix, AZ 85001
Mauricio Mendez

[2] The listings were compiled by the National Association of Spanish Broadcasters (NASB) for the study *U.S. Hispanics—A Market Profile,* edited by Antonio Guernica. The study was published by the National Association of Spanish Broadcasters and Strategy Research Corporation in 1980 and updated by NASB to January 1981.

KPHX-AM   1480 kHz   (602) 257-1351
1975 S. Central Ave., Phoenix, AZ 85004
Mozelle Butler

Tucson

KEVT-AM   690 kHz   (602) 624-5588
Box 101, Tucson, AZ 85702
Joe Crystall

KXEW-AM   1600 kHz   (602) 623-6429
889 W. El Puente Ln., Tucson, AZ 85713
Ernesto V. Portillo

CALIFORNIA

Bakersfield

KWAC-AM   1490 kHz   (805) 327-9711
5200 Standard St., Bakersfield, CA 93308
Gerry Welch

Coachella

KVIM-FM   93.7 MHz   (714) 347-2333
Drawer 401, Indio, CA 92201
Gilberto Esquivel (Program Director)

Fremont

KDOS-FM   104.9 MHz   (415) 791-1212
4510 Peralta Blvd., no. 4, Fremont, CA 94536
Inez Martinez

Fresno

KGST-AM   1600 MHz   (209) 266-9901
P.O. Box 11868, Fresno, CA 93775
Ben Gutierrez

KXEX-AM   1550 kHz   (209) 233-8803
P.O. Box 12223, Fresno, CA 93777
John Sonder

Gilroy

KAZA-AM   1290 kHz   (408) 998-1290
Box 1290, San Jose, CA 95108
Ines Castillo

Hollister

KMPG-AM   1520 kHz   (408) 637-7476
Box 1414, Hollister, CA 95023
Gilberto DeLeon

Lodi

KCVR-AM   1570 kHz   (209) 368-0626
P.O. Box 600, Lodi, CA 95240
George L. Sampson

Lompoc

KNEZ-AM   960 kHz   (805) 736-3496
322 N. H St., Lompoc, CA 93436
Lee Garza

Los Angeles

KLVE-FM   107.5 MHz   (213) 465-3171
5724 Hollywood Blvd., Los Angeles, CA 90028
Elias Lieberman

KROQ-AM   1500 kHz   (213) 387-1115
1330 S. Vermont, Los Angeles, CA 90006
José Molina

KTNQ-AM   1020 kHz   (213) 465-3171
5724 Hollywood Blvd., Los Angeles, CA 90028
Elias Lieberman

McFarland

KXEM-AM   1590 kHz   (805) 792-2128
P.O. Box 326, McFarland, CA 93250
Joe Hochschild

Ontario

KNSE-AM   1510 kHz   (714) 981-8893
P.O. Box 5000, Ontario, CA 91761
Jack L. Siegal

Oxnard

KOXR-AM   910 kHz   (805) 487-0444
418 W. Third St., Oxnard, CA 93030
Norman L. Posen

Pasadena

KWKW-AM   1300 kHz   (213) 466-8111
6777 Hollywood Blvd., Hollywood, CA 90028
José Cabrera

Redlands

KCAL-AM   1410 kHz   (714) 825-5020
Box 390, Redlands, CA 92373
Andy James

Roseville

KPIP-FM   93.5 MHz   (916) 791-4111
P.O. Box 1110, Roseville, CA 95678
Gene Ragle

Salinas

KCTY-AM   980 kHz   (408) 449-2421
P.O. Box 1939, Salinas, CA 93902
Martin L. Kline, Jr.

KRAY-FM   103.9 MHz   (408) 449-2421
P.O. Box 1939, Salinas, CA 93902
Martin L. Kline, Jr.

San Francisco

KBRG-FM   105.3 MHz   (415) 626-1053
1355 Market St., San Francisco, CA 94103
Doug Matthews

KIQI-AM   1010 kHz   (415) 648-1010
2601 Mission St., San Francisco, CA 94110
Rene de la Rosa

San Gabriel

KALI-AM   1430 kHz   (213) 287-9955
1104 S. San Gabriel Blvd., San Gabriel, CA 91776
Philip A. Malkin

San Jose

KNTA-AM   1430 kHz   (408) 244-1430
P.O. Box 6528, San Jose, CA 95150
Gene Hogan

San Mateo

KOFY-AM   1050 kHz   (415) 692-2433
1818 Gilbreth Rd., Burlingame, CA 94010
Jess Carlos

Santa Maria

KZON-AM   1600 kHz   (805) 922-7323
605 W. Main, Santa Maria, CA 93454
Jim Gregori

Santa Rosa

KBBF-FM   89.1 MHz   (707) 545-8833
P.O. Box 7189, Santa Rosa, CA 95401
Josue Lopez

Stockton

KSTN-FM   107.3 MHz   (209) 948-5786
2171 Ralph Ave., Stockton, CA 95206
Nacho Moreno (Program Director)

COLORADO

Denver

KBNO-AM   1220 kHz   (303) 922-1151
1601 W. Jewell Ave., Denver, CO 80223
Edward Romero (President)

Pueblo

KAPI-AM   690 kHz   (303) 545-2883
2829 Lowell Blvd., Pueblo, CO 81003
Andres Neidig

CONNECTICUT

Hartford

WLVH-FM   93.7 MHz   (203) 549-1175
18 Asylum St., Hartford, CT 06103
José Grimalt

New Britain

WRYM-AM   840 kHz   (203) 666-5646
1056 Willard Ave., Newington, CT 06111
Barry A. Kursman

FLORIDA

Kissimmee

WMJK-AM   1220 kHz   (305) 422-7053
1200 Central Ave., Kissimmee, FL 32741
Bebo Kramer

Miami

WCMQ-AM   1220 kHz   (305) 854-1830
1411 Coral Way, Miami, FL 33145
Joseph Rey

WCMQ-FM   92.1 MHz   (305) 854-1830
1411 Coral Way, Miami, FL 33145
Joseph Rey
WHTT-AM   1260 kHz   (305) 625-4000
Box 450550, Miami, FL 33145
David Gleason
WOCN-AM   1450 kHz   (305) 371-1450
P.O. Box 1450, Miami, FL 33145
Carlos Fernandez
WQBA-AM   1140 kHz   (305) 643-5000
701 S.W. 27th Ave., Miami, FL 33135
Herbert M. Levin
WQBA-FM   107.5 MHz   (305) 643-5000
701 S.W. 27th Ave., Miami, FL 33135
Herbert M. Levin
WRHC-AM   1550 kHz   (305) 541-3300
2260 S.W. 8th St., Miami, FL 33135
Salvador Lew

Tampa
WYOU-AM   1550 kHz   (813) 253-6071
P.O. Box 1988, Tampa, FL 33601
Art Reuben

ILLINOIS

Chicago
WCRW-AM   1240 kHz   (312) 327-6860
2756 Pine Grove Ave., Chicago, IL 60614
Edward Jacker
WEDC-AM   1240 kHz   (312) 631-0700
5475 N. Milwaukee Ave., Chicago, IL 60630
A. B. Pucinski
WSBC-AM   1240 kHz   (312) 777-1700
4949 W. Belmont Ave., Chicago, IL 60641
Daniel R. Lee

Evanston
WOJO-FM   105 MHz   (312) 869-8900
2425 Main St., Evanston, IL 60202
Athena Sofios
WONX-AM   1590 kHz   (312) 475-1590
2100 Lee St., Evanston, IL 60202
Ken Kovas

Oak Park

WOPA-AM   1490 kHz   (312) 848-5760
408 S. Oak Park Ave., Oak Park, IL 60302
Sidney Schneider

LOUISIANA

Gretna

KGLA-AM   1540 kHz   (504) 347-8491
Box 428, Marrero, LA 70072
Alberto Carrillo

MARYLAND

Wheaton

WMDO-AM   1540 kHz   (301) 933-6920
2647 University Blvd. W., Wheaton, MD 20902
Allan Kramer

MASSACHUSETTS

Boston

WUNR-AM   1600 kHz   (617) 367-9003
160 N. Washington St., Boston, MA 02114
Jane Dunkley

NEW JERSEY

Millville

WREY-AM   1440 kHz   (609) 825-2600
P.O. Box 1440, South Vineland, NJ 08360
Joseph Coccaro

Vineland

WDVL-AM   1270 kHz   (609) 696-2070
Box 457, Vineland, NJ 08360
Vita Marie Ventresca

NEW MEXICO

Albuquerque

KABQ-AM   1350 kHz   (505) 243-1744
Box 4486, Albuquerque, NM 87106
Frank Elders

Espanola

KDCE-AM   970 kHz   (505) 753-2201
P.O. Box 970, Espanola, NM 87533
James F. Hoffman

Las Vegas

KNMX-AM   540 kHz   (505) 425-3555
615 Lincoln Ave., Las Vegas, NM 87701
Carlos D. Lopez

Roswell

KRDD-AM   1320 kHz   (505) 623-8111
Box 1615, Roswell, NM 88201
Joe S. Alvarez

NEW YORK

New York

WADO-AM   1280 kHz   (212) 599-2701
666 Third Ave., New York, NY 10017
Nelson Lavergne

WBNX-AM   1380 kHz   (212) 594-1380
Box 1380, Carlstadt, NJ 07072
Georgina Garcia

WJIT-AM   1480 kHz   (212) 935-5170
655 Madison Ave., New York, NY 10021
Len Mirelson

TEXAS

Austin

KMXX-FM   102.3 MHz   (512) 478-5699
121 E. 8th St., Austin, TX 78701
Martin Rosales, Jr.

Beeville

KCWW-FM   104.9 MHz   (512) 358-1490
Box 700, Beeville, TX 78102
Joe Ed Hernandez (Program Director)

Bishop

KFLZ-FM   107.1 MHz   (512) 584-2915
110 E. Main St., Bishop, TX 78343
Joe A. Cisneros

Carrizo Springs
KBEN-AM   1450 kHz   (512) 876-2210
203 S. 4th St., Carrizo Springs, TX 78834
Walter H. Herbort

Corpus Christi
KCCT-AM   1150 kHz   (512) 884-2426
701 Benys, Corpus Christi, TX 78405
Manuel Davila, Jr.

KUNO-AM   1400 kHz   (512) 884-5203
Drawer 4722, Corpus Christi, TX 78408
Luis A. Muñoz

Eagle Pass
KEPS-AM   1270 kHz   (512) 773-9246
P.O. Box 1123, Eagle Pass, TX 78852
Doug Stalker

El Paso
KAMA-AM   1060 kHz   (915) 544-7600
4150 Pinnacle St., El Paso, TX 79902
Jack R. McVeigh, Sr.

KAMA-FM   93.1 MHz   (915) 544-7600
4150 Pinnacle St., El Paso, TX 79902
Jack R. McVeigh, Sr.

Falfurrias
KPSO-AM   1260 kHz   (512) 325-2112
Box 309, Falfurrias, TX 78355
Raymond Creely

Fort Worth
KESS-FM   93.9 MHz   (817) 429-1037
Box 6195, Fort Worth, TX 76115
Marcos Rodriguez (President)

KTIA-AM   1540 kHz   (817) 336-1540
616 One Tandy Center, Fort Worth, TX 76102
Johnny Gonzales

Harlingen
KGBT-AM   1530 kHz   (512) 423-8990
P.O. Box 711, Harlingen, TX 78550
Carlos A. Cantu

KIWW-FM   96.1 MHz   (512) 423-3211
302 W. Adams, Harlingen, TX 78550
Willie Harris, Jr.

Houston

KEYH-AM   950 kHz   (713) 527-9363
3130 Southwest Freeway, Houston, TX 77098
Donald Wigginton

KLAT-FM   101.0 MHz   (713) 224-5528
1101 N. Milby Plaza, Houston, TX 77003
Ricardo Castello

KXYZ-AM   1300 kHz   (713) 472-2500
P.O. Box 87190, Houston, TX 77017
Bill Waters

Lubbock

KLFB-AM   1420 kHz   (806) 765-8114
P.O. Box 5697, Lubbock, TX 79417
Marcelo Tafoya

McAllen

KQXX-FM   98.5 MHz   (512) 686-2111
608 S. 10th St., McAllen, TX 78501
C. T. McKassen

Midland

KWEL-AM   1000 kHz   (915) 697-7300
3306 Andrew Hwy., Midland, TX 79703
Bob Hicks

Mission

KIRT-AM   1580 kHz   (512) 585-1629
6055 10th St., McAllen, TX 78501
C. T. McKassen

Odessa

KJJT-AM   1000 kHz   (915) 333-3101
1315 W. County Rd., Odessa, TX 79763
Pete Almanza

Pasadena

KLVL-AM   1480 kHz   (713) 225-3207
111 N. Ennis, Houston, TX 77003
Felix H. Morales

Pearsall

KVWG-AM   1380 kHz   (512) 334-2500
Box K, Pearsall, TX 78061
Elizabeth Sifuentes

Port Lavaca

KGUL-AM   1560 kHz   (512) 552-2951
105 Calhoun Plaza, Port Lavaca, TX 77979
Joe Carreon (Spanish Manager)

Ralls

KCLR-AM   1530 kHz   (806) 762-1314
Box 669, Ralls, TX 79357
Mickey Renteria

Rosenberg

KFRD-AM   980 kHz   (713) 342-6601
P.O. Box 832, Rosenberg, TX 77471
George Thompson

San Angelo

KSJT-FM   97.5 MHz   (915) 653-5008
Box 1296, San Angelo, TX 76901
Thomas H. Earnest

San Antonio

KCOR-AM   1350 kHz   (512) 225-2751
1115 W. Martin, San Antonio, TX 78207
Nathan Safir

KEDA-AM   1540 kHz   (512) 226-5254
510 S. Flores St., San Antonio, TX 78204
Manuel G. Davila (President)

KFHM-AM   1150 kHz   (512) 224-1166
106 S. Concho St., San Antonio, TX 78207
Angel Toledo

KUKA-AM   1250 kHz   (512) 225-5757
501 W. Quincy, San Antonio, TX 78212
Marshall Coe (President)

KVAR-FM   104 MHz   (512) 226-6444
427 E. 9th St., San Antonio, TX 78215
Everett Kunin

Taylor

KRGT-FM   92.1 MHz   (512) 255-1261
Box 6354, Austin, TX 78702
Marcelo Tafoya

Chapter 4

Television – Viewing Habits

As of the beginning of 1982 there were twelve Spanish language television stations in the United States plus a Spanish station in Houston still in the developmental stage. Of the twelve stations, ten are affiliates of SIN–National Spanish Television Network. An independent, KBSC-TV, in Los Angeles goes over the air as subscription television at night. The television stations are all in markets with high Hispanic concentration; seven of the twelve are located in the top five Hispanic population markets in the U.S.

In descending market order, Spanish language television stations operate in New York, WNJU-TV and WXTV; Los Angeles, KBSC-TV and KMEX-TV; San Antonio, KWEX-TV; Miami, WLTV; San Francisco, KDTV; Chicago, WCIU-TV; Phoenix, KTVW-TV; Fresno, KFTV; Corpus Christi, KORO-TV; and Sacramento-Stockton, KLOC-TV. SIN's network programming signal was also carried by over 100 cable systems and translators (low-power repeater stations) as of the beginning of 1982, in addition to their full-power television stations. It is expected that the number of cable systems carrying Spanish language programming will continue to grow significantly in the 1980s.

U.S. Hispanics display a strong preference for Spanish language television over English language television. Spanish stations consistently draw the largest Hispanic-audience share among the television stations in the market. It is not uncommon for Spanish television's share of the Hispanic audience to exceed 50 percent during certain

35

time periods. It is not impossible to find Hispanic household ratings of over 40 for specific programs. Hispanics, however, do spend a considerable amount of their viewing time with English language television.

The Hispanic viewing of English language television parallels the viewing patterns of the general audience in terms of program preferences and peak viewing times. The programs that draw the largest general-audience ratings also attract the largest number of Hispanics who watch English language television. It is well worth noting that even though Hispanics watch a considerable amount of English language television, their emotional affinity toward most general-audience programming and advertising is weak.

Spanish television appeals to Hispanics by offering programming in their native tongue. The dramatic characters and their behavior, the way they react to situations, are in tune with the Hispanic's cultural expectations. The program themes and the environment in which these themes evolve are also attuned to the cultural values of the Hispanic.

Spanish television serves many of the same functions for Hispanics as does Spanish radio. Spanish television serves as a primary source of news for the Hispanic concerning both the local community and the country of origin. Spanish television provides Hispanics with the feeling of belonging by supplying a familiar programming niche substantially different from the day-to-day reality of American society. As with Spanish radio, a sense of loyalty to Spanish television also exists, except that in the case of Spanish television, the loyalty is more to specific programs than to the specific station.

Most of Spanish television's programming is imported from outside the country. Spanish language television programming produced within the United States is basically limited to local news programs, public affairs presentations, talk shows, and an occasional series or special. Although SIN–National Spanish Television Network does offer a domestically produced nightly national news program and has plans for increased domestic production in the future, the bulk of the programming carried by U.S. Spanish television comes from Mexico, with Puerto Rico holding the second-place slot. Spain and Spanish-speaking countries in Central and South America also contribute an occasional series.

In a certain sense, U.S. Spanish television's Mexican slant is to be expected; Mexico produces more Spanish language programming than any other country in the world. Mexican-Americans also make up the majority of the U.S. Hispanic population. Still, although the preponderance of Mexican programming perhaps makes sense at the national level, Spanish stations in markets with little Mexican population try to balance their schedules with programming produced in Hispanic countries other than Mexico.

It is difficult to judge whether the Mexican slant in programming deters other Hispanics from tuning in and results in lower Spanish-television viewing levels among non-Mexican Hispanics. In Miami, WLTV carries primarily Mexican programming in a city with a Hispanic population that is less than 5 percent Mexican; WLTV draws some of the highest Hispanic audience shares of any television station in the United States. New York has two Spanish language television stations, WNJU-TV and WXTV, and a Hispanic population that is approximately 65 percent Puerto Rican and less than 5 percent Mexican. WNJU-TV carries primarily Puerto Rican programs and over the years has consistently drawn a larger Hispanic audience than has WXTV, which carries primarily Mexican programming. Although ethnic orientation is believed to play a substantial role, the difference in the ratings is not necessarily a function of the Mexican or Puerto Rican angle of the New York stations.

Neither the Miami nor the New York case, considered alone, is conclusive. It is safe to assume, however, that Spanish programming produced in Mexico is intended to have more direct appeal for Mexican than for non-Mexican Hispanics. Moreover, the U.S. Hispanic population is a secondary audience for any programming produced outside of the United States, regardless of the country of origin. The primary audience is the producing country's own population.

The diversity of program formats offered by Spanish television parallels that of general-audience television. During a typical broadcast week, a Spanish television station will offer situation comedies, *novelas* (soap operas), variety shows, sports, game shows, news, talk shows, children's programming, movies, and possibly a special or two. There are striking contrasts, however, between Spanish and English language television when it comes to the place that each program format occupies in their respective schedules.

The most distinctive aspect of Spanish television is the immense importance of the *novela* format. The *novela* is essentially a soap opera with a few differences. *Novelas* are not open-ended; they have a set number of episodes within each series. Some of the best-known Hispanic actors and actresses perform in *novelas* as opposed to the relative unknowns who play in English daytime soap operas.

Novelas traditionally draw the largest audience of any Spanish program format; it is primarily a female audience. *Novelas* are so highly successful with Hispanics that Spanish stations schedule them during prime time as well as during the day. It is not unusual for a Spanish television station to devote a third or more of its Monday through Friday air time to *novelas.*

While other program formats on Spanish television are secondary, they all have their place in the daily schedule of a Spanish station. During 1980 an SIN affiliate's typical programming from 9:00 A.M. until early afternoon consisted of a half hour of children's programming, a movie, a half-hour game show, an hour and a half of talk shows, and an hour's worth of *novelas.* From 2:00 P.M. SIN offered 3 solid hours of *novelas.* Following the 5:30 to 6:30 P.M. local news came a half-hour comedy, an hour and a half of *novelas,* an hour and a half of variety and comedy, and a half-hour *novela.* At 10:30 P.M. SIN stations broadcast a 1-hour international news program followed by a movie.

In all, an SIN station's typical weekday from 9:00 A.M. to 1:00 A.M. the next day during 1980 consisted of *novelas,* 6 hours; movies, 4 hours; news, 2 hours; talk shows, 1½ hours; variety shows, 1 to 1½ hours; comedies, ½ to 1 hour; game shows, ½ hour; and children's programming, ½ hour.

The number of *novelas* shown on weekends was much fewer, partly because a *novela* needs a regular time period that fits easily into a viewer's daily routine in order to be most successful. Sports programming played a large role on Saturday with a 1-hour sports review program plus 2 hours of live boxing and 2 hours of soccer, both of which are very popular Hispanic male spectator sports.

Specials play a big part in the success of Spanish television by enhancing the station's involvement in the local Hispanic community. Much of the special programming aired by Spanish stations commemorates holidays that are celebrated by Hispanics in their country of origin but that are scarcely known in the United States. These specials serve the double purpose of recognizing the local Hispanic culture and acting as a cultural reminder for young Hispanics who may be unfamiliar with the significance of the holidays.

The local Hispanic community's responsiveness to Spanish television is evident during telethons such as are held to raise money for cancer research. In Miami, the Spanish television station usually raises more contributions from the Hispanic community each year than its English counterparts do from their audiences.

Increasingly, Spanish television has begun to focus on concerns of national importance to Hispanics. In 1980, the year of the decennial census, Spanish stations took an active role in encouraging Hispanics to respond to the census by producing and broadcasting an extensive public service campaign stressing the importance of being counted in the census. The campaign included announcements from Hispanic political and entertainment celebrities and culminated on census day,

April 1, with a national special on the SIN stations, where Hispanic personalities performed and filled out the census forms on screen, giving the viewers at home instructions on how to complete them.

In 1980, Spanish stations on the SIN system also developed a year-long campaign on the national elections and the electoral process. The campaign urged Hispanics to register to vote and to use the vote, and it provided information on the candidates' stands, particularly in regard to issues that concerned Hispanics. The election campaign specials featured a monthly prime-time special on the elections and ended with live coverage on election night.

Just as specials commemorating national holidays remind U.S. Hispanics of their uniqueness in American society, specials on the census and the election process urge Hispanics toward fuller participation in the mainstream of American life. Spanish television expresses Hispanic cultural values in its programming while encouraging Hispanics to play an effective role in the society in which they live.

PROGRAM FORMATS[1]

With the exception of program formats specifically targeted at the Hispanic male, such as sports, Spanish television produces considerably higher ratings for Hispanic women 18 years of age and older than it does for Hispanic men in the same age group. Higher ratings among women appear to hold true irrespective of program formats other than sports. This is partly due to the salient role that *novelas* play on Spanish television schedules.

Novelas These make up approximately one-third of Spanish television's total broadcast time. They consistently deliver higher household (HH) ratings than any other format, showing particularly high ratings for women 18 years of age and older. They deliver ratings for men of this age group that are comparable with those obtained by any other program format, including sports. The ratio of women to men in the 18-and-older age group who watch *novelas* is approximately 1.5 to 1.

Comedies These are scheduled for approximately 1 hour each broadcast day. HH ratings are usually lower than those for *novelas;* however, the ratio of women to men in the 18-and-older age group who watch comedies is approximately the same as for *novelas* (1.5 to 1).

[1] The data on Hispanic viewing of Spanish television according to program formats was derived from personal-interview ratings surveys among Hispanics conducted by Strategy Research Corporation during 1980 and provided by SIN–National Spanish Television Network.

News (Local and International) News programming usually consists of a 1-hour local newscast in the late afternoon and a 1-hour late-night international newscast. HH ratings are lower than for *novelas,* with ratings for women barely higher than those for men in the 18-and-older age group.

Sports These are primarily scheduled for the weekends, usually Saturday, for approximately 4 hours. Soccer and boxing make up the bulk of sports programming. HH ratings are considerably lower than for *novelas,* with ratings for women and men in the 18-and-older age group basically equal.

Variety Shows These are usually scheduled in prime time for 1 hour. HH ratings are slightly lower than for *novelas* in a comparable time period. The ratings for women are higher than those for men in the 18-and-older age group, but not as much as for *novelas.* The ratio is approximately 1.3 to 1.

In markets without Spanish television, it is believed that Hispanics follow approximately the same viewing patterns as the general audience.

DAY-PARTS[2]

Hispanic HUT (households using television) levels average approximately 25 percent between noon and 4:30 P.M., 45 percent between 4:30 and 7:30 P.M., and 60 percent between 7:30 and 11:00 P.M., Monday through Friday.

Beginning at noon, the Hispanic HUT level gradually rises, making a midafternoon jump of over 5 percent around 4:00 P.M. It continues rising gradually, making a slightly bigger jump of approximately 7 percent at 6:00 P.M. Continuing its gradual rise, the Hispanic HUT level shows its greatest single increase at 8:00 P.M., jumping more than 10 percent over the previous half hour.

The 8:00 to 10:00 P.M. time slot sustains a Hispanic HUT level of approximately 65 percent, the highest peak of the day. The level drops drastically at 10:00 P.M. by over 10 percentage points.

In terms of cumulative audience, the 7:30 to 11:00 P.M., Monday through Friday time period delivers approximately 70 percent of Hispanic households. The 4:30 to 7:30 P.M. slot reaches approximately

<hr>

[2] The data on Hispanic viewing of Spanish television according to day-parts was derived from personal-interview ratings surveys among Hispanics conducted by Strategy Research Corporation during 1980 and provided by SIN–National Spanish Television Network.

60 percent of Hispanic households, with approximately 35 percent of Hispanic households tuning in at some point between noon and 4:30 P.M.

AUDIENCE COMPOSITION

In general, Hispanic women watch Spanish television more frequently and for longer periods of time than do Hispanic men. Older Hispanics are more likely to watch Spanish television than are younger Hispanics. Less affluent Hispanics also view a greater amount of Spanish television than do higher-income Hispanics. According to the 1979 Gallup telephone survey of Spanish-surname households with listed telephones, *Listening and Viewing Habits of Hispanic Americans,* approximately half of U.S. Hispanics view Spanish television at least once each weekday.

Men 18 Years of Age and Older   According to ratings surveys conducted by Strategy Research Corporation among Hispanics, the weakest day-part for reaching Hispanic men is the early-afternoon, noon to 4:30 P.M., Monday through Friday, time period. The late-afternoon time slot of 4:30 to 7:30 P.M., Monday through Friday, delivers twice the cumulative audience of men age 18 and older than does the early-afternoon time slot. The 7:30 P.M. to midnight period delivers the highest cumulative audience of men in this age group, approximately 10 percent higher than the late-afternoon time slot.

According to the Gallup study, 47 percent of Hispanic men age 18 and older watch Spanish television at some point each weekday. Up to 3 hours per weekday are watched by 34 percent of the Hispanic men, with 8 percent watching over 3 hours each weekday.

Women 18 Years of Age and Older   According to Strategy Research Corporation's ratings surveys, the 7:30 P.M. to midnight, Monday through Friday, night period delivers the largest cumulative audience of women age 18 and older, slightly less than twice that of the noon to 4:30 P.M. time slot. The 4:30 to 7:30 P.M., Monday through Friday, time slot delivers approximately 10 percent less than the night period does and 25 percent more than the early-afternoon period.

The 1979 Gallup survey shows that 51 percent of Hispanic women view some Spanish television each weekday. Approximately 12 percent watch up to 1 hour of Spanish television every weekday,

21 percent watch 1 to 3 hours, and 13 percent spend over 3 hours with Spanish television.

Teenagers (12 to 17 Years Old)   Ratings surveys conducted by Strategy Research Corporation reflect that Hispanic teenagers spend considerably less time watching Spanish television than do Hispanic adults. Less than half of Hispanic teenagers watch any amount of Spanish television during a broadcast week. The 7:30 P.M. to midnight, Monday through Friday, time period provides the highest cumulative audience of teenagers, approximately twice that of the early-afternoon slot. The late-afternoon period of 4:30 to 7:30 P.M. delivers a teenager cumulative audience of approximately 15 percentage points more than the early-afternoon slot does and less than 10 percent under that of the nighttime period.

Age Comparisons   The 1979 Gallup study reports that 45 percent of Hispanics 18 to 34 years old watch at least some Spanish television each day: 16 percent view Spanish television up to 1 hour per weekday, another 16 percent view from 1 to 3 hours, and 11 percent watch over 3 hours per weekday.

Of the 35- to 49-year-old Hispanics, Gallup found that 44 percent tune into Spanish television each weekday: 9 percent view up to 1 hour, 21 percent from 1 to 3 hours, and 10 percent watch Spanish television 3 or more hours each weekday.

Of Hispanics 50 years of age and older, 59 percent watch Spanish television each weekday: up to 1 hour is viewed by 16 percent, 1 to 3 hours by 25 percent, and over 3 hours of Spanish television are seen by 14 percent of the Hispanics surveyed in this age group.

CONCLUSION

Spanish television enjoys the same strong identification and involvement with the Hispanic community that Spanish radio enjoys, although Spanish radio's involvement is perhaps more direct and personal. The entertainment programming carried by Spanish television is culturally in touch with Hispanics and provides an informational and emotional tie to their cultural values and their countries of origin.

The characters and situations presented in most English language programming are not directly related to the Hispanic's own circumstances and behavior. In advertising, the situations and appeal used to persuade the mass market do not work as well with the Hispanic audience, partly owing to the programming environment in which they are presented.

Spanish television provides a credible and comfortable programming environment for Hispanics. Advertising presented within that environment carries a sense of inherent credibility and will elicit a strong Hispanic consumer response, from an audience that is appreciative of the advertiser's effort.

LISTINGS—SPANISH-FORMAT TELEVISION STATIONS[3]

The following list is alphabetical by state and primary coverage area. "Spanish-format television stations" are defined as those stations that broadcast for 50 percent or more of their air time in the Spanish language. Most of the stations in the list are full-time Spanish language television stations.

Key to Listings:

First line	Call letters Network Channel Telephone
Second line	Address
Third line	General manager

ARIZONA

Phoenix

KTVW-TV   (SIN)   Ch. 33   (602) 252-3833
3019 E. Southern, Phoenix, AZ 85040
Danny Villanueva, Jr.

CALIFORNIA

Hanford/Fresno

KFTV   (SIN)   Ch. 21   (209) 263-4204
1857 Fulton St., Fresno, CA 93721
Luis Romanacce

Los Angeles

KBSC-TV   (Ind.)   Ch. 52   (213) 507-6522
1139 Grand Central Ave., Glendale, CA 91201
John Mohr

[3] The listings were compiled by the National Association of Spanish Broadcasters (NASB) for the study *U.S. Hispanics—A Market Profile*, edited by Antonio Guernica. The study was published by the National Association of Spanish Broadcasters and Strategy Research Corporation in 1980 and updated by NASB to January 1981.

KMEX-TV (SIN) Ch. 34 (213) 466-8131
5420 Melrose Ave., Hollywood, CA 90038
Daniel Villanueva

Modesto

KLOC-TV (SIN) Ch. 19 (209) 527-3060
2842 Iowa Ave., Modesto, CA 95351
Chester Smith

San Francisco

KDTV (SIN) Ch. 14 (415) 641-1400
2200 Palou Ave., San Francisco, CA 94124
Emilio Nicolas, Jr.

FLORIDA

Miami

WLTV (SIN) Ch. 23 (305) 652-4000
2525 S.W. 3d Ave., no. 412, Miami, FL 33129
Joaquin Blaya

ILLINOIS

Chicago

WCIU-TV (SIN) Ch. 26 (312) 663-0260
141 W. Jackson Blvd., Chicago, IL 60604
Howard Shapiro

NEW YORK

New York

WNJU-TV (Ind.) Ch. 47 (201) 643-9100
1020 Broad St., Newark, NJ 07102
Carlos Barba

WXTV (SIN) Ch. 41 (201) 348-4141
24 Meadowland Pkwy., Secaucus, NJ 07094
Ivan Egas

TEXAS

Corpus Christi

KORO-TV (SIN) Ch. 28 (512) 883-2823
102 N. Mesquite, Corpus Christi, TX 78401
Servando Caballero

Houston

KEON-TV   (Ind.)   Ch. 20
Houston, TX
(on-air date unavailable)

San Antonio

KWEX-TV   (SIN)   Ch. 41   (512) 227-4141
P.O. Box 9225, San Antonio, TX 78204
Emilio Nicolas

THE
MARKET

PART

Chapter 5

Demographic Profile

Perhaps the most serious problem in discussing the U.S. Hispanic market is the lack of concensus as to its size, makeup, and characteristics. The 1980 decennial census placed the number of Hispanics in the United States at 14.6 million, based on self-identification according to Spanish origin. Such respected publications as *Time* and *Newsweek* have placed the U.S. Hispanic population at approximately 20 million. Other estimates argue convincingly for a Hispanic population exceeding 25 million.

Estimates of the U.S. Hispanic population ranging from 14 to 25 million are not uncommon and may actually be accurate depending on how the population being measured is operationally defined. The universe of "persons of Spanish origin in the United States" is not the same universe as "Spanish-speaking persons in the United States." A U.S. Hispanic population figure that includes Hispanic undocumented or illegal aliens in its count will differ greatly from one that does not account for that segment of the Hispanic population. Some U.S. Hispanic market figures include the population on the island of Puerto Rico as a matter of course, and others do not.

While there is great overlapping among the Spanish-speaking, Spanish-origin, Spanish-surname, and Spanish-heritage populations, they are not identical populations. A population survey based on one of these determinant factors, or on a combination of these factors, would not necessarily arrive at the same results as a population survey based on different determinant factors.

In this demographic profile, "Hispanics" are defined as persons of Spanish origin or heritage who speak Spanish. Thus, persons of Spanish surname or origin who do not speak Spanish are not included, for the most part. Since a variety of sources were utilized, however, there may have been some departure from this definition in a few cases.

For comparison purposes, a number of references in this chapter contain 1970 U.S. Bureau of the Census population figures. The definition of the Spanish population figures in the 1970 census is not consistent at the national level or, occasionally, at the regional level. In some cases the 1970 Spanish population figures may be based on surname or on self-classification according to Spanish origin. In other cases, they may be based on language spoken. It should be noted that this applies only to the 1970 Spanish population data and not to the new estimates.

No comprehensive or systematic attempt has been made to take into account the large number of Hispanic undocumented or illegal aliens in the population estimates included in this chapter. However, in some cases the population estimates may or may not include an incidental portion of this undocumented segment. Federal estimates place the size of the Hispanic undocumented alien population at approximately 7.4 million. Estimates from other sources place the Hispanic undocumented alien population at anywhere from 3 to 12 million nationwide.

WORLD RANK[1]

As of January 1, 1980, the Hispanic population of the United States was estimated at 14,974,800, making the United States the fifth-largest Hispanic nation in the world (see Table 5-1). The U.S. Hispanic population is over 40 percent larger than the population of Venezuela and approximately 70 percent larger than the population of Chile.

Were the Hispanic population of Puerto Rico to be included in the U.S. Hispanic estimate, the total would rise to 18,459,000, although the world rank would remain the same.

AGE AND SEX DISTRIBUTION

The average U.S. Hispanic is approximately 7 years younger than his or her non-Hispanic counterpart. The median age of U.S. Hispanics is 22.1 years of age as compared with a median age of 29.5 for the general population. (See Table 5-2.)

Over 40 percent of the U.S. Hispanic population is under 18 years

---

[1] All the demographic statistics that follow in this chapter were prepared by Strategy Research Corporation for the study *U.S. Hispanics—A Market Profile,* edited by Antonio Guernica and published by the National Association of Spanish Broadcasters and Strategy Research Corporation in 1980.

TABLE 5-1 U.S. Hispanic Population versus Population in Other Hispanic Countries: 1980*

Country	Population (000)	Country	Population (000)
Mexico	48,313.4	Bolivia	4,804.0
Spain	33,290.0	Dominican Republic	4,011.6
Argentina	23,983.0	Commonwealth of	
Columbia	21,117.0	Puerto Rico	3,484.2
United States	14,974.8	El Salvador	3,418.5
Peru	13,586.3	Uruguay	2,900.0
Venezuela	10,398.9	Honduras	2,495.0
Chile	8,834.8	Paraguay	2,314.0
Cuba	8,553.4	Nicaragua	1,914.0
Ecuador	6,144.0	Costa Rica	1,800.0
Guatemala	5,200.0	Panama	1,425.3

* Portugal (pop. 10 mil.) and Brazil (pop. 90 mil.) not included in definition of term "Hispanic."

SOURCE Strategy Research Corporation; Rand McNally World Atlas.

old, and over 25 percent of the U.S. Hispanic population is under 12 years of age. The comparative youth of the U.S. Hispanic population is one of the primary factors taken into consideration in projections indicating that the U.S. Hispanic population will continue growing at a much faster rate than the general population.

TABLE 5-2 Age and Sex Distribution of U.S. Hispanic Market: 1980*

	U.S. Hispanic population (000)	Percent of total U.S. Hispanic population
Males:		
18–34	2,166.5	14.5
35–49	1,076.0	7.2
50–64	639.8	4.3
65+	305.3	2.0
Total males (18+)	4,187.6	28.0
Females:		
18–34	2,454.9	16.4
35–49	1,165.7	7.8
50–64	710.2	4.7
65+	370.6	2.5
Total females (18+)	4,701.4	31.4
Teens (12–17)	1,956.2	13.1
Children (0–11)	4,129.6	27.6
Total persons	14,974.8	100.0

* Median age = 22.1.

SOURCE Strategy Research Corporation.

AREA OF ORIGIN

Of the 15 million Hispanics in the United States, 8.9 million, or 59 percent, are of Mexican origin. This is almost four times the size of the second-largest origin subgroup, Puerto Ricans (2.3 million), and eight times larger than the third Hispanic-origin segment, Central and South Americans (1.1 million). (See Table 5-3.)

The U.S. Hispanic population is regionally concentrated according to national Hispanic origin. Over 75 percent of the total U.S. Mexican-origin population resides in the southwest and Pacific regions of the United States. Over 60 percent of the total U.S. Puerto Rican population is found in New York, with another sizable Puerto Rican population living in Chicago. The Cuban population is primarily concentrated in Florida, although there is also a numerically large Cuban population in New York. The Central and South American population in the United States is geographically dispersed, although centered in the large cities, notably New York, San Francisco, Los Angeles, Chicago, and, increasingly, Miami.

Here it is interesting to note some of the findings from *Spanish USA—A Study of the Hispanic Market in the United States,* conducted by Yankelovich, Skelly & White, Inc., for the SIN–National Spanish Television Network and published in June 1981. In the area of migration history according to Hispanic origin, the *Spanish USA* study found that 53 percent of Mexican-origin Hispanics, 18 percent of Puerto Ricans, and 7 percent of Cubans and other Hispanics were born in the United States.

The fact that the U.S. Hispanic population is geographically concentrated according to national origin does not mean that in a particular area or city it is completely homogeneous. Although the degree of regional predominance of a specific Hispanic nationality is important, it would not be entirely correct to view regions or cities in purely national-origin terms.

TABLE 5-3   Area of Origin of U.S. Hispanic Population: 1980

	Number of persons (000)	Percent of total U.S. Hispanic population
Mexico	8,895.0	59.4
Puerto Rico	2,261.2	15.1
Central and South America	1,108.1	7.4
Cuba	883.5	5.9
Other	1,826.9	12.2
Total	14,974.8	100.0

SOURCE   U.S. Bureau of the Census; Strategy Research Corporation.

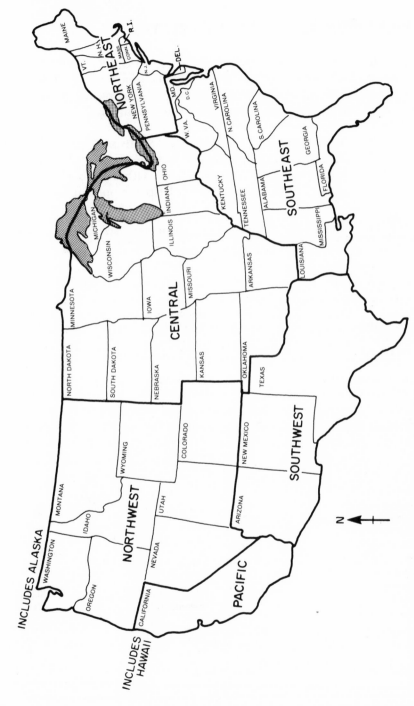

Figure 5-1 Geographic regions of the United States.

POPULATION BY REGION AND STATE

The southwest (Arizona, New Mexico, and Texas) and Pacific (California and Hawaii) regions of the United States (see Figure 5-1 for a regional breakdown) contain 8,751,700 Hispanics, representing 58 percent of the total United States Hispanic population. (See Table 5-4.) The northeast and southeast regions encompass 4,240,200 Hispanics, representing 28 percent of the total U.S. Hispanic population, with New York and Miami as the primary Hispanic population centers. The central region has 1,297,700 Hispanics within its boundaries, with over 50 percent of the central region Hispanic population resid-

TABLE 5-4   U.S. Hispanic Population by Region and State: 1980

Region and state	Population (000)	Region and state	Population (000)
Northeast	2,791.8	Kansas	56.1
Connecticut	107.5	Michigan	141.2
Maine	5.0	Minnesota	26.8
Massachusetts	81.3	Missouri	47.5
New Hampshire	3.8	Nebraska	24.5
New Jersey	534.8	North Dakota	1.9
New York	1,927.4	Ohio	112.5
Pennsylvania	120.9	Oklahoma	45.7
Rhode Island	8.5	South Dakota	3.5
Vermont	2.6	Wisconsin	47.5
Southeast	1,448.4	Southwest	4,656.8
Alabama	18.1	Arizona	530.5
Delaware	8.4	New Mexico	595.0
District of Columbia	29.9	Texas	3,531.3
Florida	1,047.6	Northwest	685.2
Georgia	40.5	Alaska	8.4
Kentucky	14.4	Colorado	380.7
Louisiana	82.7	Idaho	28.0
Maryland	69.1	Montana	7.2
Mississippi	10.9	Nevada	40.9
North Carolina	31.6	Oregon	44.9
South Carolina	15.4	Utah	54.9
Tennessee	15.3	Washington	96.8
Virginia	56.8	Wyoming	23.4
West Virginia	7.7	Pacific	4,094.9
Central	1,297.7	California	4,066.0
Arkansas	12.4	Hawaii	28.9
Illinois	670.6	Total	14,974.8
Indiana	85.6		
Iowa	21.9		

SOURCE   Market Statistics, Inc.; Strategy Research Corporation.

ing in the Chicago area. The Hispanic population in the northwest region (685,200) represents less than 5 percent of the national U.S. Hispanic population, although Hispanics are increasingly moving to the northwest.

Ten states contain 13,425,100 Hispanics, representing 90 percent of the total U.S. Hispanic population (see Table 5-4). In descending order, these states are California, Texas, New York, Florida, Illinois, New Mexico, New Jersey, Arizona, Colorado, and Michigan. The top four states—California, 4,066,000; Texas, 3,531,300; New York, 1,927,400; and Florida, 1,047,600—encompass 10.6 million Hispanics, representing 71 percent of the total U.S. Hispanic population.

HISPANIC POPULATION GROWTH, 1970 TO 1980

From 1970 to 1980 the total U.S. population grew approximately 10 percent from 203 million in 1970 to an estimated 223 million in 1980. During the same 10 years, the U.S. Hispanic population increased 65 percent, from 9 million in 1970 to 15 million in 1980, a rate approximately 6.5 times that of the general population. (See Table 5-5.)

Since the time at which these estimates were made, the U.S. Bureau of the Census has released an unadjusted 1980 census count of 226 million for the total population in the United States. An interesting sidenote in the 1980 unadjusted census count is that over 40 percent of the national population growth was attributed to just three states: California, Texas, and Florida; the first, second, and fourth states, respectively, in terms of U.S. Hispanic population. These three states showed an increase of 9.25 million people between 1970 and 1980. It is expected that Hispanics will be shown to constitute a substantial portion of this increase. The total population of New York, the state with the third-largest Hispanic population, showed little change from the 1970 figure.

TABLE 5-5   U.S. Population, Total versus Hispanic: 1970 and 1980

	1970 (000)	1980 (000)	Increase	
			(000)	(%)
Total U.S.	203,211.9	222,688.1	+19,476.2	+9.6
U.S. Hispanic	9,072.6	14,974.8	+5,902.2	+65.1

SOURCE   Market Statistics, Inc.; U.S. Bureau of the Census; Strategy Research Corporation.

HISPANIC POPULATION GROWTH BY REGION, 1970 TO 1980

All geographic regions in the United States experienced substantial growth in their U.S. Hispanic populations. Of particular note are the northeast region (131 percent growth, primarily in the New York

TABLE 5-6   U.S. Hispanic Population by Region: 1970 and 1980

Region	Population		1970–1980 growth	
	1970 (000)	1980 (000)	(000)	(%)
Northeast	1,210.5	2,791.8	1,581.3	130.6
Southeast	754.0	1,448.4	694.4	92.1
Central	894.3	1,297.7	403.4	45.1
Southwest	2,800.5	4,656.8	1,856.3	66.3
Northwest	515.9	685.2	169.3	32.8
Pacific	3,115.8	4,094.9	979.1	31.4
Total	9,072.6*	14,974.8	5,683.8	61.2

* The 1970 total Hispanic population (9072.6) is the Spanish-origin population as taken from Census Report PC(2)-1C, *Persons of Spanish Origin*. This population was determined via a closed-ended, self-classification question. Some of the limitations involving this method include:

1. Inconsistent classification of "no answers"—in the southwest, for example, if the entry was missing but the person had a Spanish surname, Mexican origin was assumed.

2. Misunderstanding—some respondents interpreted the category Central or South American to mean central or southern United States, suggesting substantial overstatement in these areas.

3. Inclusion of Portuguese-origin persons—some Brazilian-origin residents may have reported Central or South American origin and therefore were classified as Spanish-origin.

The 1970 census used three other identifiers of the Spanish population: birthplace, surname (southwest only), and language spoken.

In an effort to better estimate the 1970 Hispanic figure, Strategy Research Corporation has compiled its own 1970 county-by-county Hispanic population for the entire United States, utilizing the following sources:

1. For counties in Arizona, California, Colorado, New Mexico, and Texas, the Census Report PC(2)-1D, *Persons of Spanish Surname*, was used.

2. For the remaining state and county totals, the *County and City Data Book, 1972* was used. In this source, the Spanish identifier was persons of Puerto Rican birth or parentage (for New York, New Jersey, and Pennsylvania) and persons of Spanish language (for the remaining forty-two states and Washington, D.C.).

3. The *County and City Data Book* does not report Spanish populations for counties with less than 400 Hispanic residents. For these counties, Strategy Research Corporation included its own 1970 Spanish population estimates.

Table 5-6 includes the 1970 Hispanic population by region from this Strategy Research Corporation compilation. The Spanish population figures utilizing this source differ somewhat from the 1970 Spanish-origin population in Table 5-5. However, for consistency Table 5-6 repeats the 1970 census "origin" Spanish population total.

SOURCE   U.S. Bureau of the Census; Market Statistics, Inc.; Strategy Research Corporation.

metropolitan area) and the southeast region (92 percent growth, primarily in the Miami area).

In absolute numerical growth, the southwest region showed the greatest increase, adding 1.9 million Hispanics between 1970 and 1980. The northeast region followed closely behind, adding 1.6 million Hispanics to its 1970 total. (See Table 5-6.)

HISPANIC VERSUS TOTAL U.S. POPULATION BY REGION

The southwest region (Arizona, New Mexico, and Texas) is the most Hispanic region, both in number and Hispanic percentage of the population. More than one out of every four persons living in the southwest region are Hispanic. The pacific region (California and Hawaii) is next in number of Hispanics and percentage of the population, with Hispanics representing 16.9 percent of the total population in the region. (See Table 5-7.)

HISPANIC VERSUS TOTAL U.S. POPULATION BY STATE

Hispanics make up 6.7 percent of the total population in the United States. New Mexico is the most Hispanic state in the country with 45 percent of the state population being Hispanic. Additionally, California, Colorado, Florida, and New York all have populations that are over 10 percent Hispanic, with Texas and Arizona being more than 20 percent Hispanic. North Dakota and Tennessee are the least

TABLE 5-7   U.S. Regional Populations, Total versus Hispanic: 1980

Region	Total (000)	Hispanic (000)	Hispanic % of total
Northeast	49,383.1	2,791.8	5.7
Southeast	54,026.5	1,448.4	2.7
Central	63,965.6	1,297.7	2.0
Southwest	17,413.0	4,656.8	26.7
Northwest	13,713.8	685.2	5.0
Pacific	24,186.1	4,094.9	16.9
Total	222,688.1	14,974.8	6.7

SOURCE   Market Statistics, Inc.; Strategy Research Corporation.

TABLE 5-8 U.S. State Populations, Total versus Hispanic: 1980

State	Total (000)	Hispanic (000)	Hispanic % of total	State	Total (000)	Hispanic (000)	Hispanic % of total
Alabama	3,801.5	18.1	0.5	Nevada	691.4	40.9	5.9
Alaska	436.4	8.4	1.9	New Hampshire	898.1	3.8	0.4
Arizona	2,534.8	530.5	20.9	New Jersey	7,350.1	534.8	7.3
Arkansas	2,223.8	12.4	0.6	New Mexico	1,323.5	595.0	45.0
California	23,263.7	4,066.0	17.5	New York	17,843.3	1,927.4	10.8
Colorado	2,774.0	380.7	13.7	North Carolina	5,687.7	31.6	0.6
Connecticut	3,145.0	107.5	3.4	North Dakota	664.7	1.9	0.3
Delaware	588.8	8.4	1.4	Ohio	10,764.4	112.5	1.0
District of Columbia	671.7	29.9	4.5	Oklahoma	2,962.2	45.7	1.5
Florida	9,264.9	1,047.6	11.3	Oregon	2,498.7	44.9	1.8
Georgia	5,177.9	40.5	0.8	Pennsylvania	11,806.0	120.9	1.0
Hawaii	922.4	28.9	3.1	Rhode Island	933.9	8.5	0.9
Idaho	916.6	28.0	3.1	South Carolina	2,966.1	15.4	0.5
Illinois	11,421.9	670.6	5.9	South Dakota	706.9	3.5	0.5
Indiana	5,371.7	85.6	1.6	Tennessee	4,442.8	15.3	0.3
Iowa	2,923.8	21.9	0.7	Texas	13,554.7	3,531.3	26.1
Kansas	2,391.5	56.1	2.3	Utah	1,357.2	54.9	4.0
Kentucky	3,548.4	14.4	0.4	Vermont	498.9	2.6	0.5
Louisiana	4,031.3	82.7	2.1	Virginia	5,287.1	56.8	1.1
Maine	1,114.2	5.0	0.4	Washington	3,798.5	96.8	2.5
Maryland	4,201.2	69.1	1.6	West Virginia	1,912.5	7.7	0.4
Massachusetts	5,793.6	81.3	1.4	Wisconsin	4,742.6	47.5	1.0
Michigan	9,214.1	141.2	1.5	Wyoming	451.1	23.4	5.2
Minnesota	4,070.9	26.8	0.7	Total	222,688.1	14,974.8	6.7
Mississippi	2,444.6	10.9	0.4				
Missouri	4,912.3	47.5	1.0				
Montana	789.9	7.2	0.9				
Nebraska	1,594.8	24.5	1.5				

SOURCE Market Statistics, Inc.; Strategy Research Corporation.

58

Hispanic of the fifty states with 0.3 percent Hispanic populations. (See Table 5-8.)

HOUSEHOLD SIZE

Although some variations in household size exist according to national Hispanic origin, every major Hispanic-origin group shows a substantially larger household size than the total U.S. mean of 2.8 persons per household. (See Table 5-9.) The average household size for the U.S. Hispanic population is 3.7 persons. The larger Hispanic household size is culturally related to the extended-family tradition and the prevalence of the Catholic religion, which prohibits the practice of birth control. Among the Hispanic-origin populations, Mexicans have the largest household size (3.9 persons), and Cubans show the smallest number of persons in the household (3.3 persons).

MEDIAN INCOME BY SPANISH ORIGIN

Although the U.S. Hispanic median family income is 68 percent of the total U.S. median family income—$12,952 versus $19,116—Hispanics in the United States are the wealthiest Hispanics in the world. The opportunity for economic improvement is the primary reason why legal and illegal Hispanic immigration to the United States continues unabated.

The relation between the U.S. Hispanic median family income

TABLE 5-9 Household Size of U.S. Hispanic Market by Type of Spanish Origin: 1980 (All Values Stated as Percentages, unless Otherwise Indicated)

Household size	Mexican origin	Puerto Rican origin	Cuban origin	Other* Spanish	Total U.S. Hispanic	Total U.S. population
Total number of households (000)	2,280.7	611.1	267.7	838.6	3,998.1	78,716.2
1–2 persons	22.8	25.7	35.3	29.6	24.7	50.5
3 persons	21.6	22.1	25.8	27.7	23.7	17.8
4 persons	24.5	24.1	17.8	21.1	23.7	16.6
5 persons	16.5	17.4	17.5	10.7	14.8	8.8
6 persons	8.8	5.5	3.9	5.3	7.3	3.7
7+ persons	6.0	5.2	3.6	5.1	5.7	2.6
Mean number of persons	3.9	3.7	3.3	3.5	3.7	2.8

* Includes Central or South American and other Spanish origin.

SOURCE U.S. Bureau of the Census; Strategy Research Corporation.

TABLE 5-10   Median Family Income of U.S. Hispanic Market by Type of Spanish Origin: 1971, 1978, and 1980

	1971	1978	1980
Total Spanish origin	$ 7,379	$11,421	$12,952
Mexican origin	7,171	11,742	13,439
Puerto Rican origin	6,011	7,972	8,787
Other Spanish origin*	8,677	13,514	15,342
U.S. Total	10,474	16,786	19,116

* Includes Cuban, Central or South American, and other Spanish origin.

SOURCE   U.S. Bureau of the Census; Strategy Research Corporation.

and that of the total U.S. population has remained relatively stable from 1970 to 1980 (see Table 5-10). In 1971, Hispanic families earned 70 percent of the median income of total U.S. families, dropping slightly to 68 percent by 1978 and staying at the 68 percent level through 1980. According to Spanish origin, Puerto Rican–origin families earn 46 percent of the median family income for the total United States, with Mexican-origin families earning 70 percent and other-Spanish-origin families earning 80 percent of the total U.S. median family income in 1980.

Yankelovich's *Spanish USA* study arrived at much higher Hispanic average family income levels according to Spanish origin in 1981. The Yankelovich study found the total Hispanic average family income to be $15,900 and the U.S. total average family income to be $18,200. According to individual Spanish origin, Yankelovich found the average annual family incomes to be the following: Puerto Rican, $11,400; Mexican, $16,300; Cuban, $21,300; and other Hispanics, $16,100.

Additionally, the *Spanish USA* study found that 28 percent of all U.S. Hispanic families earn $20,000 or more. The same study indicated that 40 percent of all U.S. families earn $20,000 or more.

MEDIAN INCOME BY GEOGRAPHIC REGION

Hispanic families in the southeast region have the highest median family income ($15,681) of any geographic region, with the northeast region showing the lowest ($9368). The southwest region, with a Hispanic median family income of $12,701, comes closest to the national Hispanic median of $12,952. (See Table 5-11.)

There are striking parallels between Hispanic median family incomes in relation to Spanish origin and geographic regions. The southeast region, which encompasses the large majority of the U.S. Cuban

TABLE 5-11   Median Family Income of U.S. Hispanic Market by Region: 1980

Region	Median income
Northeast	$ 9,368
Southeast	15,681
Central	NA*
Southwest	12,701
Northwest	NA
Pacific	13,876
Total U.S. Hispanic	12,952

* Not available.

SOURCE   U.S. Bureau of the Census; Strategy Research Corporation.

population, shows the highest median family income ($15,681) and is very close to the 1980 median income ($15,342) for other-Spanish-origin families, which includes the U.S. Cuban population in its definition.

Similarly, the northeast region, in which the U.S. Puerto Rican population is concentrated, shows the lowest regional median income ($9368) and comes closest to the 1980 Puerto Rican median income ($8787). The southwest ($12,701) and Pacific ($13,876) regions, with primarily Mexican-origin Hispanic populations, approximate both the 1980 Mexican-origin ($13,439) and the total Spanish-origin ($12,952) median family incomes.

EDUCATION

Of the Hispanic population 25 years of age and older, 43.1 percent have completed 4 years of high school or more as compared with approximately 65 percent of the total U.S. population in that age group. Examining the educational level of U.S. Hispanics ages 20 to 24, the rising educational attainment of the Hispanic population becomes evident. Among Hispanics 20 to 24 years old, 63.9 percent have completed 4 years of high school or more. In fact, 28 percent of these 20- to 24-year-olds have completed at least 1 to 3 years of college. (See Table 5-12.)

It should be remembered that over 40 percent of the U.S. Hispanic population is under 18 years of age. Given the expected increase in educational opportunities for Hispanics, the level of Hispanic educational attainment should rise significantly during the 1980s.

Significant differences in educational attainment are evident according to Spanish origin. Among the various Spanish-origin populations 25 years of age and older, the other Spanish-origin group has

TABLE 5-12   Education Level of U.S. Hispanic Population by Age and Type of Spanish Origin: 1980 (All Values Stated as Percentages, unless Otherwise Indicated)

Age and type of Spanish origin	Total (000)	Elementary school			High school		College	
		0–4	5–7	8	1–3	4	1–3	4 or more
Total Spanish origin (14+)	10,199	11.8	15.5	9.3	22.3	24.6	10.9	5.6
14–19	1,870	2.6	13.3	18.1	50.5	12.7	2.8	
20–24	1,544	3.0	8.2	4.6	20.5	35.7	26.1	2.1
25+	6,785	16.0	17.8	8.1	15.0	25.4	9.8	7.9
Mexican origin (14+)	5,933	15.2	17.5	8.4	22.0	23.7	9.7	3.5
14–19	1,085	3.9	13.6	17.7	50.6	13.0	1.3	
20–24	1,023	3.3	10.8	5.2	20.1	39.4	20.3	1.3
25+	3,825	21.5	20.6	6.7	14.4	22.6	9.4	4.9
Puerto Rican origin (14+)	1,478	10.1	14.6	12.2	29.5	22.9	7.8	3.1
14–19	307	2.4	14.6	20.4	53.0	7.2	2.5	
20–24	166	(B)*	(B)	(B)	(B)	(B)	(B)	(B)
25+	1,005	13.7	16.5	9.9	21.0	28.2	6.9	4.2
Other Spanish origin† (14+)	2,786	5.1	11.7	9.9	19.5	27.4	15.3	11.5
14–19	478	0.5	12.0	16.9	48.3	14.7	7.4	
20–24	354	2.2	2.6	1.2	15.2	32.2	42.1	4.5
25+	1,954	6.9	13.0	10.0	13.2	29.7	12.2	15.6

* Represents base of less than 80,000.

† Includes Cuban, Central or South American, and other Spanish origin.

SOURCE   Strategy Research Corporation; U.S. Bureau of the Census.

reached the highest level, with 57.5 percent having completed at least 4 years of high school as compared with 39.3 percent of the Puerto Rican and 36.9 percent of the Mexican populations.

Of the Spanish-origin populations between 20 and 24 years of age, the other-Spanish-origin group is also the highest, with 78.8 percent having completed at least 4 years of high school as compared with 61 percent of the Mexican population and 63.9 percent of the total Spanish-origin population. The educational level of Puerto Ricans between 20 and 24 years of age is not available.

Among the total Spanish-origin population 25 years of age and older, there is little difference in educational achievement at the high school level between males and females. (See Table 5-13.) In this age group, 44.4 percent of the total Spanish-origin male popula-

TABLE 5-13 Education Level of U.S. Hispanic Population by Sex, Age, and Type of Spanish Origin: March 1980 (All Values Stated as Percentages, unless Otherwise Indicated)

Age and type of Spanish origin	Total (000)	Elementary school			High school		College	
		0–4	5–7	8	1–3	4	1–3	4 or more
Male								
Total Spanish origin (14+)	4,866	10.5	15.0	10.0	22.8	22.7	12.7	6.4
14–19	946	1.9	11.3	21.1	53.4	10.5	1.9	
20–24	742	1.5	9.3	4.5	15.8	35.7	31.2	2.2
25+	3,178	15.0	17.5	8.1	15.2	23.4	11.6	9.4
Mexican origin (14+)	2,891	13.7	17.1	9.4	21.2	23.6	11.7	3.3
14–19	513	3.3	9.6	23.4	52.2	11.3	0.5	
20–24	492	2.8	12.2	4.5	17.6	39.0	23.3	0.9
25+	1,886	19.2	20.8	7.0	13.7	22.9	11.9	4.8
Puerto Rican origin (14+)	640	8.6	13.7	13.2	32.3	19.6	10.0	2.8
14–19	160	2.4	18.9	17.1	52.1	9.5		
20–24	73	(B)*	(B)	(B)	(B)	(B)	(B)	(B)
25+	407	13.7	12.9	10.2	24.6	24.2	10.1	4.6
Other Spanish origin† (14+)	1,335	4.2	11.1	10.0	21.5	22.2	16.2	15.0
14–19	273	—	10.8	18.6	54.1	9.0	7.3	
20–24	177	—	3.0	—	6.6	33.7	49.5	7.2
25+	885	6.7	12.6	9.6	14.0	24.2	12.0	21.0
Female								
Total Spanish origin (14+)	5,333	13.0	15.9	8.7	21.9	26.4	9.3	4.8
14–19	924	3.4	15.4	15.0	47.6	15.0	3.7	
20–24	802	4.5	7.1	4.6	24.8	35.8	21.3	2.0
25+	3,607	17.1	18.0	8.1	14.9	27.2	8.2	6.6
Mexican origin (14+)	3,043	16.7	17.9	7.4	22.7	23.8	7.9	3.7
14–19	572	4.4	17.2	12.6	49.2	14.6	2.0	
20–24	531	3.8	9.5	5.9	22.4	39.7	17.6	1.6
25+	1,940	23.7	20.5	6.4	15.1	22.3	6.9	5.1
Puerto Rican origin (14+)	838	11.2	15.3	11.4	27.3	25.5	6.2	3.3
14–19	147	2.3	9.9	23.9	54.0	4.8	5.2	
20–24	93	(B)	(B)	(B)	(B)	(B)	(B)	(B)
25+	598	13.7	18.9	9.7	18.5	31.0	4.7	3.9
Other Spanish origin† (14+)	1,452	5.9	12.2	9.8	17.7	32.2	14.4	8.2
14–19	205	1.2	13.6	14.8	40.5	22.3	7.6	
20–24	178	4.4	2.2	2.4	23.7	30.7	34.8	1.8
25+	1,069	7.0	13.4	10.3	12.6	34.2	12.3	11.1

* Represents base of less than 80,000.
† Includes Cuban, Central or South American, and other Spanish origin.

SOURCE   Strategy Research Corporation; U.S. Bureau of the Census.

tion have completed at least 4 years of high school as compared with 42 percent of the females. The difference becomes more pronounced when examining college education, with 21 percent of the Spanish-origin males 25 years old and older having completed at least 1 to 3 years of college as compared with 14.8 percent of the females.

Differences in educational attainment are also discernible along Spanish-origin lines. Among the male and female Spanish-origin groups 25 years of age and older, the other-Spanish-origin group far outdistances the Mexican- and Puerto Rican–origin groups. In this age group, 57.2 percent of other-Spanish-origin males have completed high school as opposed to 39.6 percent of the Mexican males and 38.9 percent of the Puerto Rican males. Among females age 25 and older, 57.6 percent of the other-Spanish-origin group have completed high school as compared with 39.3 percent of the Puerto Rican females and 34.3 percent of the Mexican females.

In the 20- to 24-year-old age group, every Spanish-origin group shows much higher educational attainment than does the 25-and-older age group, while differences remain constant according to the type of Spanish origin.

EMPLOYMENT

The leading occupational category for the total Spanish-origin population in the United States is that of operatives and laborers (blue collar), accounting for 34.9 percent of the jobs Hispanics hold (see Table 5-14). The second-highest occupational category is that of service workers, accounting for 17.3 percent of the jobs. The combination of these two occupational categories represents 52.2 percent of the jobs held by the Spanish-origin population.

As is the case with income and education, there are significant differences in the type of employment according to Spanish origin. Of the Cuban-origin working population 34 percent hold positions in the occupational category of professional, technical, and kindred workers and in the category of managers and administrators, as compared with 18.9 percent of the other-Spanish-origin, 14.6 percent of the Puerto Rican–origin, and 12.2 percent of the Mexican-origin working populations.

One of the basic differences in Hispanic employment patterns according to sex is the level of employment among males 16 years old and older, as compared with their female counterparts. (See Table 5-15.) In this age group, 77.6 percent of the Hispanic males are employed, as compared with 43.1 percent of the Hispanic females.

TABLE 5–14   Employment of U.S. Hispanic Population by Type of Spanish Origin and Employment Category: 1980 (All Values Stated as Percentages, Unless Otherwise Indicated)

	Spanish origin				
	Mexican	Puerto Rican	Cuban	Other*	Total
Total number of persons 16 years old and older (000)	5,541	1,265	523	2,117	9,446
Total number of employed (000)	3,411	597	385	1,209	5,602
Occupation:					
Professional, technical, and kindred workers	6.7	9.1	17.9	12.3	8.9
Managers and administrators	5.5	5.5	16.1	6.6	6.5
Sales workers	4.0	6.6	4.6	4.7	4.3
Clerical and kindred workers	12.9	24.0	12.3	13.4	14.3
Craft and kindred workers	16.6	9.9	10.6	8.8	13.8
Operatives and laborers	38.4	33.3	22.0	30.3	34.9
Service workers	16.2	11.9	16.5	23.9	17.3

* Includes Central or South American and other Spanish origin.

SOURCE   Strategy Research Corporation.

Differences in the first two employment categories in Table 5-15 according to Spanish origin are particularly accentuated among males. Of the Cuban-origin males working, 43.4 percent hold positions as professional, technical, and kindred workers or as managers and administrators, as compared with 22 percent of the other-Spanish-origin, 11.7 percent of the Mexican-origin, and 10.6 percent of the Puerto Rican–origin males working.

The category of operatives and laborers is the largest category by far, encompassing 40.3 percent of the jobs held by Spanish-origin males. The second-largest category is craft and kindred workers, with 21.8 percent of the jobs held by Spanish-origin males.

Female employment in the first two employment categories in Table 5-15 is much more uniform than male employment across Spanish-origin lines. Of the Puerto Rican–origin females working, 21.3 percent are employed as professional, technical, and kindred workers or as managers and administrators, as compared with 21.2 percent of the Cuban-origin females, 14.4 percent of the other-Spanish-origin females, and 13 percent of the Mexican-origin females. Of the total Spanish-origin females working, 77.4 percent hold jobs as clerical and kindred workers, as operatives and laborers, or as service workers in closely descending order.

TABLE 5–15 Employment of U.S. Hispanic Population by Sex, Type of Spanish Origin, and Employment Category: 1980 (All Values Stated as Percentages, unless Otherwise Indicated)

	Spanish origin				
	Mexican	Puerto Rican	Cuban	Other*	Total
	Male				
Total number of persons 16 years old and older (000)	2,694	522	219	1,005	4,440
Total number of employed (000)	2,136	372	228	708	3,444
Occupation:					
Professional, technical, and kindred workers	5.1	7.5	20.8	14.2	8.3
Managers and administrators	6.6	3.1	22.6	7.8	7.7
Sales workers	2.3	4.8	1.7	3.5	2.8
Clerical and kindred workers	4.9	14.9	0.9	4.1	5.6
Craft and kindred workers	26.1	15.0	14.8	14.3	21.8
Operatives and laborers	43.3	39.2	28.9	36.4	40.3
Service workers	12.1	15.6	10.3	19.7	13.5
	Female				
Total number of persons 16 years old and older (000)	2,847	743	304	1,112	5,006
Total number of employed (000)	1,275	225	157	501	2,158
Occupation:					
Professional, technical, and kindred workers	9.2	11.7	14.2	9.8	10.0
Managers and administrators	3.8	9.6	7.0	4.6	4.9
Sales workers	6.4	9.3	9.1	5.8	6.8
Clerical and kindred workers	26.1	39.3	27.8	26.4	28.0
Craft and kindred workers	0.8	1.3	4.5	0.5	0.9
Operatives and laborers	31.2	23.2	13.3	22.6	26.3
Service workers	22.7	5.6	24.3	30.3	23.1

* Includes Central or South American and other Spanish origin.

SOURCE Strategy Research Corporation.

METROPOLITAN VERSUS NONMETROPOLITAN RESIDENCE

The Hispanic population of the United States is overwhelmingly concentrated in metropolitan areas (see Table 5-16). Of all U.S. Hispanics, 86.5 percent live within metropolitan areas, as compared with approximately 66 percent of the non-Hispanic population of the United

TABLE 5–16   Residence in Metropolitan versus Nonmetropolitan Areas for U.S. Hispanic Population by Type of Spanish Origin: 1980

	Mexican	Puerto Rican	Other* Spanish	Total U.S. Hispanic
Total number of families (000)	2,280.7	611.1	1,106.3	3,998.1
Metropolitan areas	83.3%	95.6%	88.0%	86.5%
Nonmetropolitan areas	16.7%	4.4%	12.0%	17.5%

* Includes Cuban, Central or South American, and other Spanish origin.

SOURCE   Strategy Research Corporation.

States. Puerto Ricans are the Spanish-origin group that is most drawn to the city, with 95.6 percent of U.S. Puerto Ricans living within metropolitan areas.

TOP THIRTY HISPANIC MARKETS

The U.S. Hispanic population is not only heavily urban and geographically concentrated according to Spanish origin, it is also concentrated

TABLE 5–17   Top Thirty Hispanic ADIs: 1980

Rank	ADI	Hispanic population (000)	Rank	ADI	Hispanic population (000)
1	New York	2,329.8	19	Tucson	182.1
2	Los Angeles	2,256.8	20	Austin	139.8
3	San Antonio	849.6	21	Tampa–St. Petersburg	133.2
4	Miami	767.4	22	Lubbock	128.7
5	San Francisco	705.8	23	Salinas-Monterey	108.6
6	Chicago	660.1	24	Laredo	106.9
7	McAllen-Brownsville	533.8	25	Odessa-Midland	104.2
8	El Paso	474.3	26	Colorado Springs–Pueblo	102.5
9	Albuquerque	465.6	27	Washington, D.C.	100.0
10	Houston	459.4	28	El Centro–Yuma	79.5
11	Phoenix	311.6	29	Detroit	70.8
12	Fresno	298.6	30	Waco-Temple	67.7
			Total		12,955.6
13	Corpus Christi	293.8			
14	San Diego	278.6	Top thirty as a percentage of		
15	Sacramento-Stockton	274.4	total U.S. Hispanic population		86.5%
16	Dallas–Fort Worth	257.0			
17	Denver	232.0			
18	Philadelphia	183.0			

SOURCE   Strategy Research Corporation.

in relatively few markets in comparison with the non-Hispanic population. Over 85 percent of the U.S. Hispanic population is found within the top thirty Hispanic areas of dominant influence (ADIs).[2] Over 60 percent of the U.S. Hispanic population (9,502,000) resides within the top ten Hispanic ADIs. An astounding 31 percent of the total U.S. Hispanic population lives in the New York and Los Angeles ADIs. (See Table 5-17.)

UNITED STATES–MEXICO BORDER MARKETS

The U.S. Hispanic market extends outside of the United States. Along the nearly 2000 miles that make up the United States–Mexico border there are 2.8 million Mexican nationals that do a great deal of their shopping on the United States side. Legal crossings at the United States–Mexico border number 82 million people per year, or almost a quarter of a million persons per day. The Mexican government has estimated that 90 percent of the Mexican population living on the border shops regularly on the U.S. side.

In a certain sense, the United States–Mexico border is merely a political line that physically separates economically interdependent cities on each side of the border. The five major pairs of cities in descending order of combined population size are El Paso ADI–Juarez, Mexico (1,074,300); McAllen-Brownsville ADI–Matamoros, Mexico (983,800); San Diego ADI–Tijuana, Mexico (918,600); El Centro-Yuma ADI–Mexicali, Mexico (629,500); and Laredo ADI–Nuevo Laredo, Mexico (331,900). (See Table 5-18.) Similar, but smaller, twin cities on the border are Nogales, Arizona–Nogales, Mexico; Douglas, Arizona–Agua Prieta, Mexico; Presidio, Texas–Ojinaga, Mexico; Del Rio, Texas–Acuña, Mexico; Eagle Pass, Texas–Piedras Negras, Mexico; and Rio Grande, Texas–Camargo, Mexico.

The twin cities are not only economically joined; they share telephone service and readily accept both U.S. and Mexico currencies. Moreover, they share a common history, culture, and custom while being somewhat dissociated from the interiors of the United States and Mexico.

The economic connection is readily evident upon examination of some consumer spending indicators. During 1978, store sales in Laredo, Texas came to approximately $470 million, or more than $6000 for each of Laredo's 76,900 residents. Laredo's per capita income

---

[2] "Areas of dominant influence," as defined by Arbitron in their media audience estimate studies, include U.S. counties and exclude non-U.S. areas.

TABLE 5–18   U.S.–Mexico Border Market Hispanic Populations: 1980

Market	Number of Hispanic persons
El Centro–Yuma ADI	79,500
Mexicali, Mexico	550,000+
El Centro–Yuma–Mexicali	629,500+
El Paso ADI	474,300
Juarez, Mexico	600,000+
El Paso–Juarez	1,074,300+
Laredo ADI	106,900
Nuevo Laredo, Mexico	225,000+
Laredo–Nuevo Laredo	331,900+
McAllen-Brownsville ADI	533,800
Matamoros, Mexico	450,000+
McAllen-Brownsville-Matamoros	983,800+
San Diego ADI	278,600
Tijuana, Mexico	640,000+
San Diego–Tijuana	918,600+

SOURCE Mexican government census update; Strategy Research Corporation.

for 1978 was $3575; obviously, the bulk of the sales was made to Mexican nationals. Laredo holds the 348th position for total consumer spendable income of all U.S. metropolitan areas while ranking 288th in total retail sales and 2d in total retail sales per household.

Similar shopping patterns hold true for the other border markets. Mexican nationals cross the border into the United States daily to buy American-made goods which they believe to be superior to those made in Mexico. While the exact amount of money spent by Mexican nationals in U.S. border stores has not been documented, the profitable and marked effect of their trade on retail sales is enjoyed daily by shopkeepers on the U.S. side.

CONCLUSION

As of 1980, there were approximately 15 million Hispanics living in the United States, that is, people who speak and comprehend the Spanish language and are of Spanish origin or descent. There is currently an additional population of undocumented Hispanic aliens, loosely estimated to be between 3 and 12 million, about whom few reliable statistics are available. Federal estimates place the size of this population at approximately 7.4 million. The United States is the fifth-largest "Hispanic country" in the world.

The median family income of U.S. Hispanics is $13,000, substantially less than the $19,000 median figure for all U.S. families. Nevertheless, U.S. Hispanics are the most affluent Hispanics in the world. For 1980, their projected gross income represented a market of approximately $51.8 billion (over $70 billion, if the undocumented population is taken into account).

From 1970 to 1980, the U.S. Hispanic population grew at a rate 6.5 times that of the general population. The average U.S. Hispanic is approximately 7 years younger than his or her non-Hispanic counterpart. The median age of U.S. Hispanics is 22.1 years, as compared with a median age of 29.5 years for the general population. Over 40 percent of the U.S. Hispanic population is under 18 years old, and over 25 percent is under 12 years of age. Their comparative youth is a primary factor in projections that indicate that the U.S. Hispanic population will continue to grow at a much faster rate than the U.S. population as a whole. Another contributing factor is the substantially larger Hispanic household size; the average size is 3.7 persons as compared with the U.S. mean of 2.8 persons per household.

Of Hispanics 25 years of age and over, 43.1 percent have completed 4 years of high school or more, as compared with approximately 65 percent of the total U.S. population in that age group. However, among younger Hispanics, ages 20 to 24, 63.9 percent have completed 4 years of high school or more. In fact, 28 percent of these 20- to 24-year-olds have completed at least 1 to 3 years of college. The average level of Hispanic educational attainment should rise significantly during the 1980s as many younger Hispanics advance through school and college.

The U.S. Hispanic population is overwhelmingly concentrated in the metropolitan areas of the country. Of all U.S. Hispanics, 86.5 percent live within metropolitan areas, as compared with 66 percent of the non-Hispanic population.

Of the 15 million U.S. Hispanics, 8.9 million, or 59 percent, are of Mexican origin. This is almost four times the size of the Puerto Rican–origin subgroup (2.3 million) and eight times larger than the Central and South American–origin Hispanic segment (1.1 million). Cuban-origin Hispanics number 883,500. Hispanics designated as being of other Spanish origin number 1.8 million.

The U.S. Hispanic population is regionally concentrated according to national Hispanic origin. Over 75 percent of the U.S. Mexican-origin population resides in the southwest and Pacific regions. Over 60 percent of the U.S.-mainland Puerto Rican–origin population is found in New York, with another sizable segment living in Chicago. The Cuban-origin population is primarily concentrated in Florida, with significant numbers in New York as well. The Central and South American–origin population is geographically dispersed, although centered in the large cities, notably New York, San Francisco, Los Angeles, Chicago, and, increasingly, Miami.

The demographic characteristics that the U.S. Hispanic population shares at the national level generally hold true at the regional and local market levels as well.

Chapter 6

The Hispanic Presence

The Hispanic presence on the North American continent has been felt for more than 3½ centuries. U.S. Hispanics descend from the native Indian cultures that ruled the new world before the arrival of the Europeans, from the original pioneers and Spanish explorers who first came to the new world, and from the west African slaves brought to cultivate the land. This combination of Indian, Iberian, and west African influences shapes the character of the U.S. Hispanic, creating a common bond while concurrently fostering diversity. Much more recently, the American influence has also contributed to the character of the U.S. Hispanic.

Throughout history, it has been the Spanish culture that has played the dominant role in shaping the character of U.S. Hispanics. When the Spanish explorers came to the new world, they brought with them the Spanish language and a deep desire to spread the Catholic religion. Both their language and their religion continue to be vibrantly alive in U.S. Hispanics today and characterize them above other cultural considerations.

In 1492, when Columbus sailed for the new world with the financial support of the Spanish Crown, the motivation was essentially economic, to seek new and more efficient trade routes to the far east. Today, the large number of Hispanics who immigrate to the United States each year come primarily with the hope of economic improvement. In a larger sense, Hispanics come to the United States to better their lives. They bring with them a willingness to work to attain that better life, and they bring with them a sense of history. The histories of Mexico, Puerto Rico, Cuba, and the United States have been intertwined for centuries, as is natural for such close neighbors. The present role of the U.S. Hispanic population in American society is inexorably tied to its history.

MEXICO

Spaniards first made contact with Mexico in the early part of the sixteenth century. In 1512, survivors of an expedition headed by Diego de Nicuesa first sighted the Yucatán peninsula. A later expedition led by Hernán Cortéz reached the shores of Mexico in 1519. On May 3 of that year, Cortéz established the city of Veracruz. From there he set out to conquer the Aztec empire. In 1522, Cortéz was appointed governor of Mexico, which he renamed New Spain. Shortly thereafter, word of newfound wealth reached the Iberian peninsula, and scores of Spaniards began arriving in the new world.

The exploration and colonization of new regions spread rapidly. By 1525, Spanish rule extended as far south as Guatemala and Honduras. In 1536, Alvar Nuñez Cabeza de Vaca explored and colonized northwest Mexico and what is now the southwest United States. In 1540, Francisco de Coronado crossed over to Oklahoma, Colorado, Kansas, and Nebraska in an unsuccessful search for gold. In 1574, long before the English established their first successful colony in the new world, the Spanish population in the city of Mexico was well beyond 15,000 inhabitants. At that time, more than 200 cities and towns were already established in Mexico, and a university was founded in Mexico City. By the end of the seventeenth century, settlements were established throughout the northern region of what was then Mexico, including present-day Texas, Arizona, California, and New Mexico.

In 1598, all land north of the Rio Grande was formally claimed for Spain by Don Juan de Onate. During the first half of the seventeenth century twenty-five settlements and missions were established in what is now the southwest United States. Spanish was spoken in the region for over 100 years before the Pilgrims landed at Plymouth, Massachusetts, in 1620. In 1609, 2 years after the first English colony was established in Jamestown, Virginia, the Spanish founded the city of Santa Fe. Spain had established twenty-one missions along the California coast by 1769, 7 years preceding the independence of the thirteen American colonies. Spanish exploration and settlement in what is now the southwest United States continued into the early part of the nineteenth century.

With the establishment of new pioneer clusters throughout the northern territory, distinct social characteristics began to emerge as a result of restricted communication with central New Spain (Mexico). Isolation between settlements and constant adjustment to the new surroundings also played an important role in the development of regional uniqueness.

In 1821, Mexico declared its independence and annexed all of Spain's colonial domains north of Rio Bravo and Rio Grande, including Texas, Arizona, Nevada, Utah, and Colorado. The years that followed Mexican independence saw an increase in trade taking place between the new Mexican republic and the United States, with whom Mexico shared a common frontier.

The increased trade with northern Mexico was greatly spurred by the opening of the Santa Fe trail, extending from Independence, Missouri, to Santa Fe. Clipper ships from New England, sailing around South America to California, also contributed to this trade. As a result, the fledgling United States came into further contact with Hispanic cultural, political, and economic influences.

Eager to expand and develop this trade, Mexico encouraged American settlements in the southwest. Mexico also hoped that the new American settlers would become loyal to Mexico and act as a buffer against the expanding United States. In 1821, the Mexican government provided Moses Austin, a St. Louis banker, with a land grant to settle Americans in what is now Texas. Within 10 years, non-Hispanic Americans outnumbered Mexicans 4 to 1.

The new settlers resisted adoption of Mexican customs and remained loyal to the United States government. Consequently, the American settlers rebelled against Mexican domination and ultimately seceded from Mexico in 1836 as the Lone Star Republic. Nine years later, in December 1845, the Lone Star Republic became part of the United States, annexed as the state of Texas. Mexico refused to recognize Texan independence or its subsequent annexation.

The following year, 1846, U.S. military troops invaded and occupied northern Mexico as far west as California and as far south as Mexico City during the U.S.-Mexican war of 1846 to 1848. Through the Treaty of Guadalupe Hidalgo, signed in 1848, the United States officially gained one-third of Mexico's total territory at that time in exchange for $15 million. This area encompassed what is now Arizona, California, New Mexico, Texas, and parts of Colorado, Nevada, and Utah. Finally, the Gadsden Purchase of 1853 established the United States–Mexico border. With the land, the United States gained approximately 75,000 Mexican settlers living in this territory, the first true Mexican-Americans.

During the rest of the nineteenth century, western, non-Hispanic American immigrants became the majority of the population while transforming the Mexican settlers into an unwelcome minority. Only in New Mexico did the Mexican settlers maintain numerical majority into the 1900s.

The Mexican settlers in the southwest United States were stripped of much of their land by the ever-growing demands of the western migration. Although Mexican property rights were theoretically protected by the Treaty of Guadalupe Hidalgo, this protection was virtually nonexistent in practice. Concurrent with the loss of land came losses in Mexican political and economic power as well as social standing. Mexicans were increasingly segregated occupationally and residentially. Nevertheless, they maintained contact with Mexico and preserved Mexican social and cultural values. Migration from Mexico also continued during this time, augmenting the Mexican population.

Migration to the United States

After 1848, new industries began to flourish; railroads were being built, cotton planted, and farms irrigated. As the need arose for cheap, mobile labor, the United States began hiring Mexican laborers. Mexicans worked on the railroad tracks and in the mines of Arizona and New Mexico. They harvested fruits in Texas and California and worked in the packing plants and the sugar beet fields of Colorado, Montana, Michigan, and Ohio.

Between 1850 and 1910, the United States was concerned with restricting oriental immigration, and not much attention was paid to Mexico. Border patrols were nonexistent, and no restrictive measures were taken to curtail movement across the United States–Mexico border. The Mexican Revolution of 1910 to 1920 spurred Mexican migration to the United States. Mexicans were eager to escape the violence in their country and to take advantage of the increasing economic opportunities in the United States.

During World War I, in order to meet emergency needs and a shortage of manpower, the U.S. government admitted a large number of Mexicans to the country on a temporary basis under the highly sensitive Immigration and Nationality Act (INA) of 1917. After the war, foreign agricultural workers continued to be hired under the INA. Permanent visas were granted to nearly half a million Mexicans during the 1920s, representing 11 percent of the decade's total U.S. immigration. Additional thousands made their way into the United States illegally during this time.

The great depression of the 1930s temporarily halted Mexican migration to the United States. Faced with a tremendous labor surplus, the United States initiated the repatriation program, leading to the emigration of approximately half a million people.

The coming of World War II saw the resumption of large-scale

Mexican immigration to the United States. When the war broke, the shortage of workers became so critical that a number of statutes were enacted to waive virtually any restrictions on the importation of foreign labor. In 1942, the United States and Mexico signed a formal agreement governing the importation of Mexican labor to the United States—the Bracero Agreement. Appropriation of government funds was also facilitated for contracting hired help. From 1942 to 1947, over 200,000 Mexican workers were employed in twenty-four states. Mexican laborers working in the fields and farms of the southwest began to move to urban areas, where they found jobs in factories, manufacturing companies, and war-related industries.

Although the Bracero Agreement was scheduled to end in 1947, it was extended to 1950 partly because of pressures from the growers. In 1951, owing to the labor demands caused by the Korean war, the Bracero program was reestablished. During this time the Mexican government established recruiting centers throughout Mexico for those seeking work in the United States. Here, potential *braceros* were examined and transported to a U.S. receiving center where a contract was drawn between employer and *bracero*. The *braceros* were to be guaranteed employment for 75 percent of the contract period, satisfactory free housing and sanitary facilities, employment insurance, free transportation back to Mexico, and the regional minimum wage. In practice, many of these guarantees were not fulfilled.

Following the postwar period, industrial growth, technological advances, and mechanization contributed to the decrease of farms and farm workers. However, the number of migrant workers increased, resulting in fierce competition among domestic and Mexican migrant workers for a shrinking job market. Finally, in 1964, the Bracero program was terminated. During the 22-year period from 1942 to 1964, more than 4.5 million Mexicans were brought legally to work on U.S. farms.

The Bracero program both encouraged and discouraged illegal Mexican migration. Drawn by the pull of wages higher than could be obtained in Mexico, the Mexican worker was very much attracted by the Bracero program, especially since it provided a formal structure. Certainly, illegal migration to the United States would have been much higher from 1942 to 1964 had the Bracero program not been in effect. However, if the Mexican worker could not enter through the Bracero program, the illegal route to the higher wages in the United States was still available.

The back-and-forth migration across the border encouraged by the Bracero program contributed to giving the crossing of the United States–Mexico border the historical casualness that it has retained to the present day.

During 1977, the Immigration and Naturalization Service caught and deported nearly 1 million illegal entrants. It is believed that close to 1 million Mexican illegal aliens enter the United States each year, virtually all of them across the United States–Mexico border.

For the Mexican government, illegal migration to the United States was and continues to be a ready safety valve for Mexican workers discontent with the lack of economic opportunities in their country. Notwithstanding its inherent problems, illegal Mexican migration provides the United States with a cheap labor supply willing to take menial and socially unattractive employment. Legal and illegal Mexican immigration to the United States will endure until such time as the two countries can offer relative parity in terms of economic opportunity.

PUERTO RICO

Puerto Rico's close association with the United States has its roots in the end of the eighteenth century. The United States had recently won its independence and had a great interest in establishing sources of trade. The close proximity of Puerto Rico and Cuba made them natural choices. Trade between Puerto Rico and the United States developed so quickly that the United States soon rivaled Spain in trade importance with the island. By the end of the eighteenth century, there were thirty-four towns in Puerto Rico and a population exceeding 150,000.

On September 23, 1868, an army of approximately 300 Puerto Ricans proclaimed independence for the island in what is known as the *Grito de Lares,* but the army was quickly defeated by Spanish soldiers. In 1897, Puerto Rico was granted autonomy by Spain through the Charter of Autonomy, which gave governing power to an island government. However, the impending Spanish-American War of 1898 hardly gave autonomy time to develop. In July 1898, American troops landed in Puerto Rico, and the United States acquired Puerto Rico through the Treaty of Paris.

The island again reverted to colony status and was under military domination by the United States. Military control ended in April 1900 through the enactment of the Foraker Act, which established free trade between the island and the United States and placed Puerto Rico under the American monetary system and tariff provisions. In 1917, the Jones Act replaced the Foraker Act, granting American citizenship to the Puerto Ricans and providing them with protection under the Bill of Rights. During World War I, the draft was instituted on the island.

During the postwar period, American economic influence on the island grew tremendously, to the point where the United States essentially controlled the island's economy. In 1947, the American government gave Puerto Rico the right to elect its own governor, previously appointed by the United States. In 1948, Luis Muñoz Marín became the first elected governor of Puerto Rico. In 1950, Puerto Rico was authorized by the U.S. Congress to draft its own constitution. Finally, on July 25, 1952, Puerto Rico was transformed from an American territory to a commonwealth, a status it still retains.

Commonwealth status links Puerto Rico to the United States through common citizenship, common defense, common currency, and common market. However, Puerto Ricans do not pay federal taxes and are denied voting representation in the U.S. Congress. Almost without exception, the same federal rules and regulations that applied to Puerto Rico as a territory apply to Puerto Rico as a commonwealth.

Migration to the United States

Few Puerto Ricans migrated to the United States prior to the end of World War II, in which they served as American soldiers. According to the U.S. Bureau of the Census, there were 1513 Puerto Ricans on the mainland in 1910. In 1940, less than 70,000 Puerto Ricans were residing on the mainland. By 1950, however, the Puerto Rican population on the mainland reached 300,000, a population more than four times greater than that in 1940. By 1960, the figure had climbed to 887,000 Puerto Ricans on the U.S. mainland.

The reason for the Puerto Rican migration to the U.S. mainland was primarily economic. The ease of the migration was greatly facilitated by regular and inexpensive air service between San Juan and New York and by the Puerto Rican's American citizenship.

During the 1950s the United States mainland offered urban jobs that were scarce on the island and that were viewed by Puerto Ricans as a step up from agricultural work. U.S. recruiters came to the island offering Puerto Ricans jobs on the mainland, particularly in New York. In the 1950s, over 400,000 Puerto Ricans migrated to the U.S. mainland, close to 20 percent of Puerto Rico's population at the time. Each year during that decade, an average of 41,000 Puerto Ricans left the island for the United States.

The 1960s saw increased industrial development in Puerto Rico, but the island economy still could not provide sufficiently attractive employment in comparison with the United States. The rate of Puerto Rican migration to the mainland lessened to an average of 20,000 people per year during the 1960s.

The downturn in the U.S. economy during the early 1970s caused a reversal in the migration flow. From 1970 to 1975 more Puerto Ricans returned to the island each year than came to the mainland.

The constant travel between the United States and Puerto Rico which began after World War II continues today. Most adult Puerto Ricans on the island have traveled at least once to the United States. According to the U.S. Census Bureau, the combined population of Puerto Ricans on the island and the mainland exceeded 4.1 million in 1970; 66 percent lived on the island, 20 percent resided in New York City, and 14 percent lived on the rest of the U.S. mainland, concentrated in urban centers.

CUBA

The drive toward Cuban independence has its origin in the first half of the nineteenth century, when numerous, though unsuccessful, attempts were made by the Cubans to gain independence from Spain. Attempts at independence continued into the second half of the nineteenth century, when on October 10, 1868, Carlos Manuel de Cespedes spearheaded the *Grito de Yara*, beginning 10 years of war between Cuba and Spain. The war ended in 1878 without the Cubans gaining independence.

During the 1800s, American economic interest in Cuba grew to the point where the United States developed a vested interest in an independent Cuba. In 1880, Spain promised to abolish slavery and to introduce political and economic reforms in Cuba, but the promises were not kept. Once again Cuba's thoughts turned to independence. José Martí, exiled in the United States, organized the Cuban Revolutionary party in 1892 together with Máximo Gómez and Antonio Machado and began planning a new revolt. Spain suspended constitutional guarantees, and war broke out on February 24, 1895.

In 1897, the Cubans elected a premier, and Spain again promised autonomy. Negotiations were to be held between Cuba and Spain. U.S. President McKinley offered to serve as mediator, but Spain refused. Before negotiations could get under way, the U.S. battleship *Maine* was blown up in Havana harbor. The American government accused Spain of the explosion and declared war on Spain on April 21, 1898, proclaiming Cuba's right to independence.

The Spanish-American War ended December 10, 1898, with the signing of the Treaty of Paris. Spain relinquished Puerto Rico, Guam, and the Phillipines to the United States and recognized Cuba's independence. The United States established military rule in Cuba, lasting to May 20, 1902. This period saw the development of public works and sanitation plants as well as advancements in education and public administration.

On June 21, 1901, the Platt amendment to the Cuban constitution was imposed. The amendment specified that Cuba would continue the public works begun by the U.S. military government and would lease naval stations to the United States. The Platt amendment also guaranteed the United States the right to intervene in Cuba's affairs if the island's independence was in jeopardy.

Cuba prospered under the new government. Sugar plantations reopened, trade with the United States was reestablished, and the island became a popular tourist spot. Closer relations developed between the two countries. In 1902, elections were held under the new constitution, and Tomás Estrada Palma was elected the first president of the new republic. In 1903, the United States opened the naval base in Guantanamo. In 1906, Tomás Estrada Palma resigned the presidency, and Cuba found itself in the midst of a political crisis. The United States intervened and stayed until 1909 when the new president, José Miguel Gómez, took power.

In 1925, Gerardo Machado was elected president. His attempts to assume dictatorial power met great opposition. The Cuban economy suffered greatly, and Cubans came to the United States as exiles. In 1933, Machado was forced out of the country, and in 1934, Fulgencio Batista established a military junta. A series of short-lived, provisional governments followed. Batista was elected president in 1940, and a new constitution was enacted on October 10 of that year.

When World War II broke out, Cuba joined the Allies. In 1952, Batista overthrew the existing government and won the presidential election of 1954 as the only candidate. Opposition to the Batista regime grew, led by Fidel Castro.

Migration to the United States

On December 31, 1958, Batista fled the country, and Castro's revolutionary forces took over the government. During the years preceding Batista's overthrow, most Cubans were encouraged by Castro's efforts and expected a democratic government when he took power. Few Cubans anticipated his communist direction, and so, few left the country prior to his victory. Once it became evident to the Cuban people that Castro would take the new government in a communist direction, a massive exodus began primarily toward the United States.

In violent disagreement with the Castro regime, the upper and middle classes began leaving the country. The Cuban exiles were prohibited by the Castro regime from taking anything of value with them. Their property and possessions became the property of the government upon their departure. Between 1961 and 1965, 177,700 Cubans registered in the refugee center of Miami.

In 1962, the United States severed diplomatic relations with Cuba as a direct result of the missile crisis. In 1965, Cuba's economic problems led Castro to declare that all Cubans were free to leave the island if they so desired. President Johnson then authorized the "freedom flights," bringing 270,000 Cubans to Miami between 1965 and 1973. Many more Cubans came by boats originating in Miami. Still others entered the United States after brief stays in Mexico, Spain, and Puerto Rico. From 1961 to 1978, over 445,000 Cubans registered in the refugee center in Miami.

The arrival in Miami of such large numbers of Cubans in such a short period of time, all leaving Cuba for the same reason, created instant Cuban communities. The Cuban population in exile shared a communal sense of identity and values. The skills that Cubans brought with them were immediately utilized to start businesses and to begin developing the economic structure and security most of them had previously enjoyed. Cubans made it a point to support Cuban businesses and establishments. They naturally gravitated to areas populated by other Cubans.

At the same time, Cubans began to make their presence felt in the general community. They revitalized Miami, changing it from primarily a tourist spot to an important bank center and economic bridge to Latin America. The degree of economic success currently enjoyed by U.S. Cubans is largely due to the professional, administrative, and financial skills they brought with them in their exile and to their willingness to put those skills to work.

In 1980, Castro again allowed large numbers of Cubans to leave the island, largely because of serious economic problems in Cuba. Approximately 120,000 Cuban refugees came from Mariel, Cuba, to Miami during the early part of 1980.

THE HISPANIC IN AMERICAN SOCIETY TODAY

Being proclaimed by the general media and the general public as "soon to be the biggest minority in the United States" is a significant recognition for Hispanics. Nevertheless, the fact that Hispanics continue to be perceived as a minority in a pluralistic society, even in areas where Hispanics in fact represent the numerical majority of the population, is much more significant.

Hispanics do not perceive themselves as a minority, with all the unfortunately negative connotations that the word usually produces. Hispanics do experience cultural estrangement and isolation, and they recognize that the dominant society and language are not the same as theirs. Hispanics know they are viewed as a minority from the outside. The overwhelming majority of Hispanics perceive themselves, however, as being *different* from the dominant society but not a minor part of it. They are far from accepting the label of minority often thrust upon them.

That U.S. Hispanics have historically resisted surrender of the Spanish language and Hispanic culture is clear evidence of the pride they have in being Hispanic. Not all U.S. Hispanics have retained their language and culture. Nevertheless, the overriding interest of U.S. Hispanics has been to participate in American society rather than assimilate into it—an extremely difficult balancing trick.

History helps to explain why the Hispanic people in this country have not followed the traditional path of assimilation traveled by most other immigrant groups. First, part of what is now the United States was populated and settled by Mexicans before non-Hispanic people arrived and made the country theirs. In Texas, New Mexico, Arizona, Nevada, California, it was the non-Hispanic people who were the newcomers and the Mexicans who initially represented the established group.

Secondly, the Puerto Ricans who have come to the U.S. mainland have arrived as U.S. citizens, not as foreigners. Therefore, the impetus to become Americanized as a prerequisite for citizenship does not exist for them. That large numbers have come to the mainland within a short time and have created Puerto Rican enclaves has further diminished the immediate need of assimilation. Social and economic survival do not hinge on talking and behaving like an English-speaking American.

Unlike Puerto Rican migration, the Cuban influx to the mainland has been politically rather than economically motivated. There are similarities, nevertheless, between the two migrations. Both groups have come to the United States over a short period of time and have established their own pockets of concentration. Within these pockets, they live comfortably enough without having to make irreversible concessions to their new country. The farther that the immigrants have ventured from these pockets, the more they have changed and adapted, but there has been no pressing need for them to assimilate in order to survive economically and socially.

There have been strong legal and social pressures on the Hispanic to force him or her to assimilate. Just a few years ago in some parts of this country, it was against the law to speak Spanish in public schools. When not ignored by the general media, Hispanics have been consistently and negatively stereotyped. Discrimination against Hispanics seeking employment or housing was commonplace 20 years ago; it is not unheard of today. In general, it has been the differences between Hispanics and other Americans, and the negative aspects of those differences, that have been and continue to be emphasized. Still, Hispanics choose not to surrender their heritage and language. In fact, they have demonstrated a disinterest in assimilating.

This disinterest has brought about both positive and negative repercussions. Hispanics have retained their cultural identity but at the expense of being perceived as a minority and as outsiders. Nevertheless, Hispanics are making great progress in increasing their participation in American society as a whole.

The forces that have been determinant throughout the history of Hispanics in this country—Spanish language retention, adherence to Catholicism, close family ties, desire to better one's life, and geographic concentration—influence U.S. Hispanic participation today. They will continue to play a major role in determining the future of U.S. Hispanics as a people and as a market.

Chapter 7

Consumer Behavior

The U.S. Hispanic population constitutes a market with a gross income exceeding $51.8 billion a year and a potential consumer goods market conservatively estimated at $30 billion. Were Hispanic undocumented aliens (estimated at 7.4 million) to be added, the market totals would rise to more than $70 billion in gross income and a potential consumer goods market exceeding $40 billion.

The U.S. Hispanic market has great potential for sellers of basic foods and services. It has been estimated that the average U.S. Hispanic family spends between 4 and 10 percent more than the average non-Hispanic family on food and other consumer items. On food alone, the U.S. Hispanic family spends approximately one-fourth more of its disposable income than does the non-Hispanic family; the lower income and larger size of the Hispanic family account for a large part of this difference.

Owing to the comparative youth of the U.S. Hispanic population, 62 percent of their spending power is controlled by families with household heads under 45 years of age, as compared with 47 percent in the non-Hispanic population. The relative youth also means that Hispanics tend to spend more on children's items than their non-Hispanic counterparts.

Although Hispanics have a lower income than non-Hispanics, they place great importance on product reputation and quality. Within affordable limits Hispanics unhesitantly will pay more for what they believe is a better-quality product or brand, particularly if it is a product that will be consumed by the family. The Hispanic preference for the well-known advertised brand and Hispanic loyalty toward a favorite brand have been documented. Store brands, usually sold at a reduced price from advertised brands, tend to do poorly in Hispanic areas. Yankelovich's *Spanish USA* study, conducted for SIN in 1981, is one of the latest surveys providing clear indication of these Hispanic consumer characteristics.

Hispanics do most of their food shopping in major supermarkets, although they supplement their supermarket purchases by buying in *bodegas,* or small neighborhood stores. *Bodegas* are particularly popular among Hispanics in New York and are an important factor in product distribution. Butcher shops offering special cuts of meat usually not available in supermarkets are also important, as are bakeries and neighborhood drugstores. Hispanic reliance on *bodegas* is declining, but they retain importance as secondary stores.

Usually there is one person in the Hispanic family who makes the majority of the grocery purchases. The woman is the primary grocery buyer in approximately 70 to 80 percent of the Hispanic families, but the Hispanic male is a much more frequent grocery-buying companion than is his non-Hispanic counterpart.

Store proximity, product availability, and the steps taken by store personnel and management to facilitate shopping for Hispanic clientele are determinant factors in Hispanic patronization of a store. In terms of Hispanic brand preference, the determinant factors consist of the price and perceived reputation of the brand, together with past and present efforts to appeal specifically to the Hispanic through advertising.

CONSUMPTION INDICES[1]

This section presents usage incidences for a wide array of products in the top four U.S. Hispanic ADIs: New York, Los Angeles, San Antonio, and Miami. Household usage incidence is included for the total market, the Hispanic market, and the non-Hispanic market. Additionally, a Hispanic/non-Hispanic usage index is shown. An index of 100 indicates that Hispanic percent incidence and non-Hispanic percent incidence are identical. An index above 100 indicates incidence among Hispanic households is higher than among non-Hispanic households.

[1] The product consumption tables for New York, Los Angeles, San Antonio, and Miami were provided by Strategy Research Corporation for the study *U.S. Hispanics—A Market Profile,* edited by Antonio Guernica and published by the National Association of Spanish Broadcasters (NASB) and Strategy Research Corporation in 1980. The "national" product consumption tables were derived from the product consumption data of the individual cities.

TABLE 7-1 Hispanic Consumption of Foods and Beverages—New York

Product	Percent of households using product			Use index, Hispanic/ non-Hispanic ratio (%)
	Total market	Hispanic	Non-Hispanic	
Baby food	11.6	18.9	9.3	203.2
Beer	50.2	62.3	46.4	134.3
Bread, white	85.8	93.4	83.5	111.9
Cereal, cold	83.8	85.5	83.2	102.8
Cheese, sliced/packaged	93.0	91.1	93.6	97.3
Chewing gum	67.3	74.7	64.8	115.3
Coffee, decaffeinated	41.3	27.3	45.4	60.1
Coffee, freeze-dried/instant	51.7	43.6	54.1	80.6
Coffee, ground	75.9	87.2	72.2	120.7
Frozen dinners, main course	26.8	23.9	27.7	86.3
Fruit, canned	76.5	84.1	74.2	113.3
Fruit nectar	29.2	66.5	17.7	375.7
Fruit-type drinks, nonpowdered	60.7	78.3	55.1	142.1
Juices, frozen	70.7	77.5	68.4	113.3
Lunch meat/cold cuts, packaged	48.3	42.3	49.9	84.8
Malt liquor	8.7	14.9	6.6	225.8
Margarine	84.5	94.2	81.6	115.4
Mayonnaise	94.6	92.4	95.2	97.1
Oil, salad/cooking	95.4	96.4	94.9	101.6
Pastries, frozen	31.4	33.1	30.7	107.8
Pet food, cat	10.4	8.0	11.1	72.1
Pet food, dog	17.6	8.1	20.5	39.5
Powdered breakfast or children's drink	30.9	48.0	25.4	189.0
Rice, natural (short/long grain)	94.6	99.7	92.9	107.3
Salad dressing, prepared	63.7	42.6	70.4	60.5
Snacks (chips, pretzels, etc.)	71.2	73.0	70.5	103.6
Soft drinks, diet	44.6	21.2	51.8	40.9
Soft drinks, regular	77.7	92.6	73.2	126.5
Soup	80.0	85.2	78.2	109.0
Spaghetti, canned	23.3	57.9	12.7	455.9
Spaghetti, dry	90.1	92.9	89.2	104.2
Spaghetti, prepared	50.3	65.1	45.8	142.1
Tomato paste, canned	65.2	68.7	64.0	107.3
Tomato sauce, canned	81.7	92.4	78.5	117.7
Tuna, canned	92.3	79.7	95.9	83.1
Vegetables, canned	73.3	79.7	71.2	111.9
Vegetables, frozen	72.5	45.4	80.9	56.1
Yogurt	49.8	40.3	52.6	76.6

SOURCE Strategy Research Corporation.

TABLE 7-2 Hispanic Consumption of Health and Beauty Aids—New York

Product	Percent of households using product			Use index, Hispanic/ non-Hispanic ratio (%)
	Total market	Hispanic	Non-Hispanic	
Baby oil	34.5	38.0	33.4	113.8
Baby powder	56.4	34.4	63.0	54.6
Deodorants	92.0	98.6	89.9	109.7
Facial/eye makeup	67.5	71.4	66.2	107.9
Hair coloring	34.6	44.8	31.4	142.7
Hair conditioner	54.0	72.2	48.4	149.2
Hair spray	50.6	44.1	52.5	84.0
Headache remedies	90.1	93.7	88.8	105.5
Indigestion and upset stomach remedies	78.4	92.7	74.0	125.3
Mouthwash	79.4	89.9	76.0	118.3
Shampoo	95.3	97.8	94.6	103.4
Toothpaste	98.7	99.7	98.3	101.4

SOURCE Strategy Research Corporation.

TABLE 7-3 Hispanic Consumption of Cleaners and Paper Goods—New York

Product	Percent of households using product			Use index, Hispanic/ non-Hispanic ratio (%)
	Total market	Hispanic	Non-Hispanic	
Bar soap	98.5	94.0	100.0	94.0
Dishwashing detergent	89.6	97.8	86.9	112.5
Drain openers	50.9	50.9	50.8	100.2
Floor wax/cleaners	47.6	65.2	42.1	154.9
Furniture wax	83.9	72.1	87.2	82.7
Insecticides	64.6	85.2	58.2	146.4
Laundry detergent	99.2	100.0	98.9	101.1
Liquid household cleaners	93.9	92.9	94.2	98.6
Oven cleaners	77.3	82.7	75.5	109.5
Paper towels	95.8	98.0	94.9	103.3
Pine oil disinfectants	64.4	92.4	55.6	166.2
Room deodorizers	76.5	83.0	74.4	111.6
Sandwich bags, plastic	60.2	49.7	63.2	78.6
Scouring powder	98.3	98.0	98.3	99.7
Toilet tissue	100.0	100.0	100.0	100.0

SOURCE Strategy Research Corporation.

TABLE 7-4   Miscellaneous Hispanic Consumption—New York

Product	Percent of households using product			Use index, Hispanic/ non-Hispanic ratio (%)
	Total market	Hispanic	Non-Hispanic	
After-shave lotion	67.5	69.0	67.1	102.8
Automobile tires	36.9	17.3	42.7	40.5
Cameras	79.3	67.0	83.1	80.6
Razor blades	74.7	75.6	74.4	101.6
Shaving cream	70.0	67.6	70.6	95.8
Television sets	98.2	96.9	98.6	98.3
Watches	90.3	85.5	91.5	93.4

SOURCE   Strategy Research Corporation.

New York

New York is the top Hispanic ADI in the United States, with a Hispanic population of 2,329,800. The New York Hispanic population represents 15.6 percent of the total U.S. Hispanic population. According to the U.S. Census Bureau, the New York Hispanic population is 60.4 percent Puerto Rican, 28.4 percent of other Spanish origin including Central and South Americans, 10.4 percent Cuban, and 0.8 percent Mexican. According to Strategy Research Corporation, 58.8 percent of New York Hispanics speak mostly Spanish at home, with 37.7 percent speaking English and Spanish equally. The New York Hispanic market has a projected gross income of between $6 to $8 billion.

Tables 7-1 to 7-4 show New York ADI Hispanic consumption patterns relative to non-Hispanic consumers.

Los Angeles

Los Angeles is the second-largest Hispanic ADI in the United States, with a Hispanic population of 2,256,800. The Los Angeles Hispanic population encompasses 15.1 percent of the total U.S. Hispanic population. In terms of Spanish origin, the U.S. Census Bureau estimates that the Los Angeles Hispanic population is 79.8 percent Mexican, 12.6 percent of other Spanish origin including Central and South Americans, 4 to 7 percent Cuban, and 2.9 percent Puerto Rican. According to Strategy Research Corporation, nearly 60 percent of Los Angeles Hispanics speak primarily Spanish at home, with approximately 33 percent speaking English and Spanish equally. The Los Angeles Hispanic market enjoys a projected gross income of approximately $8 billion.

Tables 7-5 to 7-8 show Los Angeles ADI Hispanic consumption patterns relative to non-Hispanic consumers.

TABLE 7-5   Hispanic Consumption of Foods and Beverages—Los Angeles

Product	Percent of households using product			Use index, Hispanic/ non-Hispanic ratio (%)
	Total market	Hispanic	Non-Hispanic	
Baby food	11.4	18.1	7.9	229.1
Beer	55.6	68.8	52.9	130.1
Bread, white	68.2	90.6	63.7	142.2
Cereal, cold	85.6	85.6	85.6	100.0
Cheese, sliced/packaged	92.4	84.9	93.9	90.4
Chewing gum	62.7	81.1	59.1	137.2
Coffee, decaffeinated	42.0	33.7	43.6	77.3
Coffee, freeze-dried/instant	50.9	62.2	48.6	128.0
Coffee, American-type, ground	61.7	49.8	63.9	77.9
Coffee, Latin-type, ground	23.4	23.4	0.0	NA*
Frozen dinners, main course	35.1	39.1	34.3	114.0
Fruit, canned	75.1	80.5	73.9	108.9
Fruit nectar	26.4	70.2	17.7	396.6
Fruit-type drinks, nonpowdered	51.4	76.9	46.1	166.8
Juices, frozen	74.4	56.2	77.9	72.1
Lunch meat/cold cuts, packaged	72.0	77.2	70.9	108.9
Malt liquor	6.2	12.0	4.9	244.9
Margarine	87.0	91.2	85.9	106.2
Mayonnaise	92.4	87.8	93.3	94.1
Oil, salad/cooking	94.3	84.5	96.3	87.7
Pastries, frozen	30.8	35.9	29.6	121.3
Pet food, cat	25.4	10.3	28.3	36.4
Pet food, dog	46.3	18.7	51.8	36.1
Powdered breakfast or children's drink	31.4	47.0	28.3	166.4
Rice, natural (short/long grain)	86.2	96.6	83.9	115.1
Salad dressing, prepared	77.8	62.9	80.6	78.0
Snacks (chips, pretzels, etc.)	69.2	72.4	68.6	105.5
Soft drinks, diet	46.6	24.4	50.9	47.9
Soft drinks, regular	62.9	87.5	57.9	151.1
Soup	88.9	91.2	87.3	104.5
Spaghetti, canned	21.0	40.4	16.9	239.1
Spaghetti, dry	88.2	92.6	87.3	106.1
Spaghetti, prepared	43.2	53.3	41.3	129.1

* Not available.
SOURCE   Strategy Research Corporation.

TABLE 7-6 Hispanic Consumption of Health and Beauty Aids—Los Angeles

Product	Percent of households using product			Use index, Hispanic/ non-Hispanic ratio (%)
	Total market	Hispanic	Non-Hispanic	
Baby oil	32.9	37.5	31.9	117.6
Baby powder	30.4	35.2	29.3	120.1
Deodorants	92.6	95.2	91.9	103.6
Facial/eye makeup	69.6	71.4	69.3	103.0
Hair coloring	29.8	33.8	28.9	117.0
Hair conditioner	50.9	45.2	51.9	87.1
Hair spray	49.5	46.9	49.9	94.0
Headache remedies	87.4	92.9	86.3	107.6
Indigestion and upset stomach remedies	72.2	92.6	67.9	136.4
Mouthwash	75.1	91.9	71.6	128.4
Shampoo	92.5	96.9	91.6	105.8
Toothpaste	98.5	99.6	98.3	101.3

SOURCE Strategy Research Corporation.

TABLE 7-7 Hispanic Consumption of Cleaners and Paper Goods—Los Angeles

Product	Percent of households using product			Use index, Hispanic/ non-Hispanic ratio (%)
	Total market	Hispanic	Non-Hispanic	
Bar soap	99.0	99.3	98.9	100.4
Dishwashing detergent	94.1	97.6	93.3	104.6
Drain openers	51.4	52.3	51.3	101.9
Floor wax/cleaners	54.7	69.4	51.6	134.5
Furniture wax	83.5	74.1	85.3	86.9
Insecticides	56.2	63.0	54.9	114.8
Laundry detergent	97.7	100.0	97.3	102.8
Liquid household cleaners	90.5	82.2	91.9	89.4
Oven cleaners	70.6	68.1	70.9	96.1
Paper towels	95.2	87.2	96.6	90.3
Pine oil disinfectants	56.0	89.2	49.3	180.9
Room deodorizers	58.1	69.1	55.9	123.6
Sandwich bags, plastic	76.2	60.3	79.3	76.0
Scouring powder	97.8	96.9	97.9	99.0
Toilet tissue	100.0	100.0	100.0	100.0

SOURCE Strategy Research Corporation.

TABLE 7-8 Miscellaneous Hispanic Consumption—Los Angeles

| Product | Percent of households using product | | | Use index, Hispanic/ non-Hispanic ratio (%) |
	Total market	Hispanic	Non-Hispanic	
After-shave lotion	67.4	80.4	64.7	124.3
Automobile tires	71.6	51.3	75.6	67.9
Cameras	85.7	52.6	92.3	57.0
Radios (including car radios)	98.9	96.6	99.3	97.3
Razor blades	70.2	78.7	68.5	114.9
Shaving cream	59.7	76.0	56.2	135.2
Television sets	99.2	96.9	99.6	97.3
Watches	90.5	84.8	91.6	92.6

SOURCE Strategy Research Corporation.

TABLE 7-9 Hispanic Consumption of Food and Beverages—San Antonio

| Product | Percent of households using product | | | Use index, Hispanic/ non-Hispanic ratio (%) |
	Total market	Hispanic	Non-Hispanic	
Baby food, jar	6.5	9.0	4.0	225.0
Beer	53.0	47.0	59.0	79.7
Bread, white	90.0	95.0	85.0	111.8
Cereal, cold	84.5	86.0	83.0	103.6
Chewing gum	70.0	75.0	65.0	115.4
Coffee, freeze-dried/instant	46.5	56.0	37.0	151.4
Coffee, ground	62.0	56.0	68.0	82.4
Frozen dinners, main course	23.0	20.0	26.0	76.9
Fruit, canned	85.0	79.0	91.0	86.8
Fruit nectar	18.0	22.0	14.0	157.1
Fruit-type drinks, nonpowdered	53.0	63.0	43.0	146.5
Juices, frozen	68.0	56.0	80.0	70.0
Lunch meats/cold cuts, packaged	74.0	79.0	69.0	114.5
Malt liquor	7.0	10.0	4.0	250.0
Mayonnaise	91.5	93.0	90.0	103.3
Oil, salad/cooking	82.5	73.0	92.0	79.3
Powdered breakfast or children's drinks	53.5	57.0	50.0	114.0
Rice, natural (short/long grain)	93.5	97.0	90.0	107.8
Salad dressing, prepared	72.0	59.0	85.0	69.4
Sandwich bags, plastic	63.0	61.0	65.0	93.8
Snacks (chips, pretzels, etc.)	82.0	85.0	79.0	107.6
Soft drinks, diet	37.5	30.0	45.0	66.7
Soft drinks, regular	73.5	80.0	67.0	119.4
Tomato paste, canned	50.0	37.0	63.0	58.7
Tomato sauce, canned	91.0	91.0	91.0	100.0
Vegetables, canned	81.5	78.0	85.0	91.8
Vegetables, frozen	63.0	44.0	82.0	53.7

SOURCE Strategy Research Corporation.

TABLE 7-10 Hispanic Consumption of Health and Beauty Aids—
San Antonio

Product	Percent of households using product			Use index, Hispanic/ non-Hispanic ratio (%)
	Total market	Hispanic	Non-Hispanic	
Deodorants	94.0	91.0	97.0	93.8
Facial/eye makeup	66.0	63.0	69.0	91.3
Hair coloring	33.0	41.0	25.0	164.0
Hair conditioner	57.5	58.0	57.0	101.8
Hair spray	58.0	45.0	71.0	63.4
Hand lotion	85.0	83.0	87.0	95.4
Headache remedies	89.0	91.0	87.0	104.6
Indigestion and upset stomach remedies	74.5	85.0	64.0	132.8
Mouthwash	82.5	86.0	79.0	108.9
Panty hose	72.5	66.0	79.0	83.5
Remedies for colds, allergies, or breathing problems	72.0	81.0	63.0	128.6
Shampoo	96.0	97.0	95.0	102.1
Toothpaste	96.5	98.0	95.0	103.2

SOURCE Strategy Research Corporation.

TABLE 7-11 Hispanic Consumption of Cleaners and Paper Goods—
San Antonio

Product	Percent of households using product			Use index, Hispanic/ non-Hispanic ratio (%)
	Total market	Hispanic	Non-Hispanic	
Dishwashing liquid	96.0	94.0	98.0	95.9
Floor wax/cleaners	48.0	58.0	38.0	152.6
Insecticides	80.0	85.0	75.0	113.3
Laundry detergents	100.0	100.0	100.0	100.0
Liquid household cleaners	82.0	73.0	91.0	80.2
Oven cleaners	57.5	59.0	56.0	105.4
Paper towels	94.0	91.0	97.0	93.8
Pine oil disinfectants	73.0	92.0	54.0	170.4
Room deodorizers	79.5	80.0	79.0	101.3
Scouring powder	93.5	90.0	97.0	92.8

SOURCE Strategy Research Corporation.

TABLE 7-12   Miscellaneous Hispanic Consumption—San Antonio

Product	Percent of households using products			Use index, Hispanic/ non-Hispanic ratio (%)
	Total market	Hispanic	Non-Hispanic	
After-shave lotion	68.0	73.0	63.0	115.9
Razor blades	73.5	79.0	68.0	116.2
Shaving cream	62.5	59.0	66.0	89.4

SOURCE   Strategy Research Corporation.

San Antonio

San Antonio is the third-largest Hispanic ADI in the United States, with a Hispanic population of 849,000. San Antonio Hispanics comprise 5.7 percent of the total U.S. Hispanic population. The U.S. Census Bureau estimates that the San Antonio Hispanic population is 95.9 percent Mexican, 2 percent of other Spanish origin including Central and South Americans, 1.5 percent Puerto Rican, and 0.6 percent Cuban. According to Strategy Research Corporation, more than 50 percent of San Antonio Hispanics speak both English and Spanish, with 28 percent speaking mainly Spanish at home. The projected gross income for San Antonio Hispanics is approximately $3 billion.

Hispanic versus non-Hispanic consumption patterns for the San Antonio ADI are shown in Tables 7-9 to 7-12.

Miami

Miami is the fourth-largest Hispanic ADI in the United States, with a Hispanic population of 767,400. (The estimated 120,000 Cuban refugees who came to Miami from Mariel during the flotilla in the early part of 1980 are not included in this total.) The Miami Hispanic population represents 5.1 percent of the total U.S. Hispanic population. According to the U.S. Census Bureau, the Miami Hispanic population is 81.2 percent Cuban, 10.5 percent of other Spanish origin including Central and South Americans, 7.3 percent Puerto Rican, and 1 percent Mexican. Strategy Research Corporation estimates that over 80 percent of Miami Hispanics speak primarily Spanish at home. The projected gross income of Miami Hispanics is approximately $3.5 billion.

Hispanic versus non-Hispanic consumption patterns for the Miami ADI are given in Tables 7-13 to 17-16.

TABLE 7-13 Hispanic Consumption of Foods and Beverages—Miami

Product	Percent of households using product			Use index, Hispanic/ non-Hispanic ratio (%)
	Total market	Hispanic	Non-Hispanic	
Baby food, dry	8.1	10.7	6.8	157.4
Baby food, jar	8.9	14.4	6.2	232.3
Beer	60.5	66.4	57.5	115.5
Bread, sliced white	90.7	93.7	89.2	105.0
Cheese, sliced processed	85.4	84.0	86.1	97.6
Chewing gum	47.0	47.0	47.0	100.0
Coffee, American-type, ground	52.1	27.0	65.0	41.5
Coffee, Latin-type, ground	31.9	83.0	5.8	1,431.0
Frozen dinners	23.4	18.7	25.9	72.2
Fruit, canned	75.8	69.7	79.0	88.2
Fruit nectar	33.9	61.0	20.1	303.5
Fruit-type drinks, nonpow- dered	46.2	37.4	50.7	73.8
Gelatin/pudding, powdered	75.7	79.4	73.9	107.4
Gelatin/pudding, ready-to-eat	18.2	26.0	14.3	181.2
Juice, fruit, frozen	57.7	41.4	66.0	62.7
Juice, tomato	58.8	58.0	59.2	98.0
Juice, mixed vegetable	41.4	40.0	42.2	94.8
Lunch meat, canned	17.9	15.0	19.4	77.3
Lunch meat, packaged	49.2	33.0	57.5	57.4
Malt liquor	4.3	6.0	3.4	176.5
Malta	14.6	42.7	0.4	10,675.0
Margarine	90.3	85.4	92.9	91.9
Mayonnaise	86.0	85.4	86.4	98.8
Oil, olive	52.6	83.7	36.8	227.5
Oil, salad/cooking	86.3	86.0	86.4	99.5
Pet food, cat	12.8	4.0	17.4	23.0
Pet food, dog	39.9	34.0	42.9	79.3
Potato/corn chips	64.5	65.0	64.3	101.1
Powdered breakfast drinks	14.8	13.7	15.4	89.0
Powdered children's drinks	25.9	22.7	27.6	82.3
Rice, instant	34.6	6.4	49.0	13.1
Rice, regular (short/long grain)	83.9	96.4	77.6	124.2
Salad dressing, dry mix	17.6	6.0	23.5	25.5
Salad dressing, prepared	56.3	38.7	65.4	59.2
Shortening	51.0	22.4	65.7	34.1
Soft drinks, diet	31.2	15.0	39.5	38.0
Soft drinks, regular	78.8	90.0	73.2	123.0
Spaghetti, canned	29.7	34.0	27.6	123.2
Spaghetti, dry	78.3	71.7	81.7	87.8
Spaghetti sauce	40.7	36.4	42.9	84.9
Tea	78.3	64.4	85.4	75.4
Tomato paste, canned	56.6	39.7	65.4	60.7

TABLE 7-13 Hispanic Consumption of Foods and Beverages—Miami *(Continued)*

Product	Percent of households using product			Use index, Hispanic/ non-Hispanic ratio (%)
	Total market	Hispanic	Non-Hispanic	
Tomato sauce, canned	79.8	87.0	76.2	114.2
Tuna, canned	82.7	74.0	87.1	85.0
Vegetables, canned	72.2	62.4	77.3	80.7
Vegetables, frozen	68.4	45.0	80.3	56.0
Yogurt	33.5	33.7	33.4	100.9

SOURCE   Strategy Research Corporation.

TABLE 7-14 Hispanic Consumption of Health and Beauty Aids—Miami

Product	Percent of households using product			Use index, Hispanic/ non-Hispanic ratio (%)
	Total market	Hispanic	Non-Hispanic	
Arthritis remedies	18.1	19.7	17.4	113.2
Cold remedies, tablets/capsules	36.2	25.0	41.9	59.7
Cold remedies, liquid	30.0	29.4	30.3	97.0
Cough syrup	40.2	37.0	41.9	88.3
Deodorants	90.5	99.4	86.1	115.5
Disposable diapers	10.7	10.0	10.9	91.7
Eye makeup	55.5	67.7	49.4	137.0
Hair coloring	35.4	48.0	29.0	165.5
Cream hair rinse	48.1	58.4	42.9	136.1
Hair spray	55.9	64.7	51.4	125.9
Hand lotion	68.9	74.7	66.0	113.2
Headache remedies	87.5	89.7	86.4	103.8
Indigestion and upset stomach remedies	67.2	62.4	69.8	89.4
Laxatives	26.9	29.0	25.9	112.0
Lipstick	81.0	89.0	76.9	115.7
Mouthwash	76.9	77.7	76.6	101.4
Ointments and rubs	51.6	45.4	54.8	82.9
Panty hose	64.9	81.4	56.5	144.1
Shampoo	92.6	96.0	90.9	105.6
Sunburn products	28.3	20.4	32.4	63.0
Suntan lotion	32.2	32.7	32.0	102.2
Toothpaste	95.4	99.7	93.2	107.0
Vitamins	50.2	43.4	53.8	80.7

SOURCE   Strategy Research Corporation.

TABLE 7-15   Hispanic Consumption of Cleaners and Paper Goods—Miami

Product	Percent of households using product			Use index, Hispanic/ non-Hispanic ratio (%)
	Total market	Hispanic	Non-Hispanic	
Bar soap	99.4	99.7	99.4	100.3
Bleach	94.3	93.7	94.6	99.1
Dishwasher detergent	33.7	20.4	40.5	50.4
Drain openers	57.8	50.4	61.6	81.8
Facial tissue	88.2	84.4	90.2	93.6
Hand detergent	97.2	98.4	96.6	101.9
Insecticides	73.9	61.4	80.3	76.5
Laundry detergent	99.0	97.7	99.7	98.0
Liquid household cleaners	85.9	81.7	88.1	92.7
Oven cleaners	63.9	70.4	60.6	116.2
Paper towels	96.4	96.7	96.3	100.4
Pine oil disinfectants	73.0	88.7	65.0	136.5
Powdered household cleaners	96.9	94.7	98.0	96.6

SOURCE   Strategy Research Corporation.

TABLE 7-16   Miscellaneous Hispanic Consumption—Miami

Product	Percent of households using product			Use index, Hispanic/ non-Hispanic ratio (%)
	Total market	Hispanic	Non-Hispanic	
After-shave lotion	55.6	61.4	52.8	116.3
Automobile insurance	84.6	87.0	83.4	104.3
Automobile tires (12 months)	44.3	47.2	42.9	110.0
Car batteries (12 months)	32.2	34.7	31.0	111.9
Flashlight batteries	70.6	67.0	72.5	92.4
Home extermination service	39.3	39.0	39.5	98.7
Razor blades	66.4	76.0	61.6	123.4
Rent-a-car	9.8	5.0	12.3	40.7
Shaving cream	57.2	59.4	56.2	105.7
Television sets	98.3	97.7	98.7	99.0
Transistor batteries	56.1	60.7	53.8	112.8
Watches	45.0	52.6	41.2	127.7

SOURCE   Strategy Research Corporation.

TABLE 7-17 National Hispanic Consumption of Foods and Beverages

Product	Percent of Hispanic households using products
Beer	63.0
Bread, white	92.6
Chewing gum	73.5
Frozen dinners, main course	28.2
Fruit, canned	80.2
Fruit nectar	61.1
Fruit-type drinks, nonpowdered	70.6
Juices, frozen	62.4
Lunch meat, packaged	58.9
Malt liquor	12.1
Mayonnaise	90.0
Oil, salad/cooking	87.7
Rice, natural (short/long grain)	97.9
Salad dressing, prepared	51.8
Soft drinks, diet	22.9
Soft drinks, regular	88.8

SOURCE Strategy Research Corporation.

TABLE 7-18 National Hispanic Consumption of Health and Beauty Aids

Product	Percent of Hispanic households using products
After-shave lotion	72.5
Deodorants	96.5
Facial/eye makeup	69.8
Hair coloring	40.7
Hair spray	47.8
Headache remedies	92.5
Indigestion and upset stomach remedies	87.8
Mouthwash	88.6
Razor blades	77.2
Shampoo	97.2
Shaving cream	68.6
Toothpaste	99.5

SOURCE Strategy Research Corporation.

TABLE 7-19   National Hispanic Consumption
of Cleaners and Paper Goods

Product	Percent of Hispanic households using products
Dishwashing liquid	97.3
Insecticides	74.1
Laundry detergent	99.7
Liquid household cleaners	84.8
Oven cleaners	72.6
Paper towels	93.0
Pine oil disinfectants	90.8
Scouring powder	96.1

SOURCE   Strategy Research Corporation.

National Product Usage

The national Hispanic household usage incidences presented in Tables
7-17 to 7-19 are compilations, weighted according to Hispanic population size, of the Hispanic household usage incidences for New York,
Los Angeles, San Antonio, and Miami. Owing to their restriction to
these four cities, the figures presented are not "national" in the strict
sense of the word.

Additionally, the population of these four cities does not parallel
the total U.S. Hispanic population in terms of Spanish national origin.
The combined population of New York, Los Angeles, San Antonio,
and Miami is 42.6 percent Mexican, 24.8 percent Puerto Rican, 16.8
percent of other Spanish origin including Central and South Americans, and 15.7 percent Cuban, according to the U.S. Bureau of the
Census. The total U.S. Hispanic population is 59.4 percent Mexican,
19.6 percent of other Spanish origin including Central and South
Americans, 15.1 percent Puerto Rican, and 5.9 percent Cuban.

Despite these divergences according to Spanish national origin,
the combined populations of New York, Los Angeles, San Antonio,
and Miami encompass 6,203,600 Hispanics, 41.4 percent of the total
U.S. Hispanic population. The household usage incidences for the
products presented in Tables 7-17 to 7-19 should therefore provide
a valid indication of the household usage incidences for these products
in the total U.S. Hispanic population.

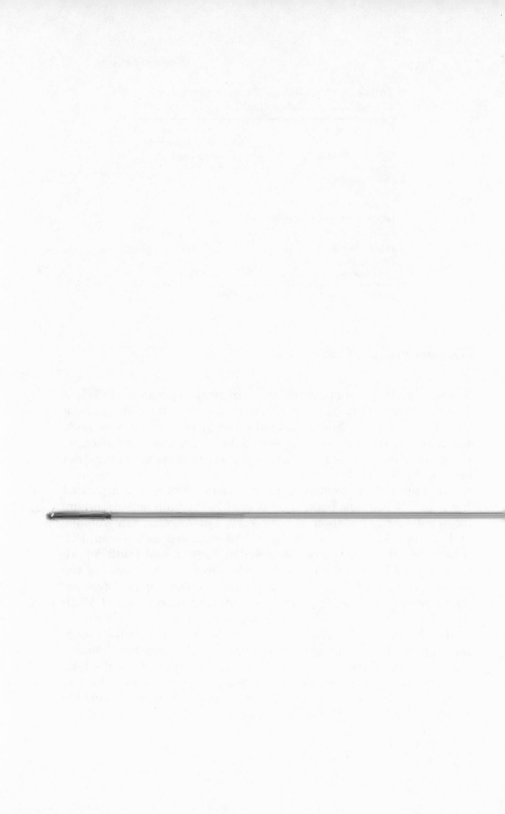

THE
METHODS

PART

Chapter 8

Making the Decision

Most advertisers think that they have enough problems holding on to their share of the general market without seriously considering entering the U.S. Hispanic market. After all, the U.S. Hispanic population represents 10 percent, at best, of the total population in the United States, and the advertiser is too busy as it is trying to reach the non-Hispanic 90 percent of the market.

In a typical scenario the advertiser is aware that the market exists and occasionally comes across an article on the Hispanic market while reading *Advertising Age* or *Adweek* and possibly skims through it. On one of those days, the advertiser gets a call from the southeast sales manager in Miami. During the conversation, the sales manager tells the advertiser in the home office that the regional sales force is saying that possibly they should look into Spanish advertising; then they go on to something else.

Sales meeting time rolls around, and a sales representative from Los Angeles makes the point that there are large numbers of Hispanics in his territory. The salesperson from San Antonio says that she has noticed the same thing in her territory. Some of the salespeople from El Paso, Albuquerque, Chicago, San Francisco, and even New York nod their heads in agreement. The meeting moves on to the next item on the agenda.

A few months down the road, the advertiser is having lunch with an account executive from the major advertising agency that handles the product brand. The conversation reaches a lull, and the advertiser happens to mention that the sales force has demonstrated some interest in the Hispanic market. The account executive says that it will be looked into. She calls the advertiser a few days later and says that Hispanics are being reached through the general media campaign.

Some time later the advertiser receives a call from a Hispanic advertising agency wishing to give a presentation on the market. The advertiser is not interested.

With few variations, this scenario is typical of the process through which the decision on whether to enter the Hispanic market usually becomes a nondecision.

Most advertisers who are in a position to make a corporate decision on Hispanic advertising today made their way through the ranks at a time when the Hispanic market was mostly a curiosity. Possibly, token budgets were assigned to Spanish advertising, but more in the spirit of social responsibility than as an investment. Consequently, these token budgets usually produced no discernible results.

In the scenario just described, the product manager called by the Hispanic advertising agency is already burdened with projects that are related to the general-audience campaign. There is little incentive to add still another project to the list when the Hispanic market is not perceived as a business opportunity. Moreover, the product manager is well-versed with advertising in the general market but perhaps knows next to nothing about the Hispanic market. If this is the case, the ability to utilize business judgment honed through years of experience is severely diminished in the Hispanic market—not a situation that would encourage the product manager to look into the market.

Still, the sales forces in high-Hispanic-population areas keep raising the subject, so the product manager turns to the major advertising agency, the same people who have provided sound advertising advice throughout the years—except that in this case, the major advertising agency is perhaps as ill-prepared as the client. The advertising agency's expertise lies in the general market, not in the Hispanic market.

Hispanic advertising is generally an unwanted complication for most major agencies. Moreover, it may not be in the best interest of the advertising agency to present the Hispanic market as a business opportunity. The investment of a realistic budget in Hispanic advertising could mean that funds will be diverted from the general-market budget to a Hispanic advertising agency or to the Hispanic division within the larger agency. Also, in all fairness to the major advertising agency, Hispanics do use English language media, so the general-audience campaign does reach them as the agency says.

What the agency does not say is that general-market advertising has little effect on persuading Hispanics, while an advertising campaign developed specifically for them can generate substantial dollar increases with a relatively low investment.

For the reasons given, however, advertisers, particularly the major advertisers, seldom reach the point where they can make a decision as to whether Hispanic advertising makes sense for them as a business investment. The situation is exacerbated in that the advertising decision makers' circle of personal contacts usually does not include someone who is familiar with advertising in the Hispanic market and in whom they have confidence. It is extremely difficult for the Hispanic marketer to bridge this gap of confidence and gain the decision makers' attention in order to present the Hispanic market as a concrete business opportunity.

Getting to the point where a decision based on the merits of the Hispanic market can be made requires sound information. In making that decision, however, the advertiser will discover that the same level of marketing information is not readily available about the Hispanic market that is available about the general market. This is particularly discouraging to advertisers in that they require a high degree of documentation on the Hispanic market and advertising precisely because of their unfamiliarity and low confidence level in these areas.

Sufficient data exist, however, to enable the advertiser to make a sound business decision, and more comprehensive data is being rapidly developed and compiled. Today, information on the market— its demographic characteristics, its buying and media habits, its psychographic characteristics—is readily available for the advertiser who desires it, and advertisers should demand all relevant information before making decisions.

Look at the consumption levels for the product in the Hispanic market. Does it enjoy a high level of consumption? How much does Hispanic consumption mean to the business in dollars?

Ask for documentation on Spanish media effectiveness. Do the media provide proper coverage of the markets the advertiser wants to reach? What are the costs per thousand (CPMs)?

Examine the success or lack of it for similar products advertising in the market. Are the product case histories solidly documented? How much was invested on products, and what was the return?

Study the major competitors' efforts in the Hispanic market. Are they currently advertising in the Hispanic market? Why or why not? What is their history in Hispanic advertising?

Examine the costs of the campaign should the advertiser choose to go in. What are the production costs? The media costs? The costs for research? How much does the brand share in the Hispanic market have to increase to pay out?

Once the advertisers have the answers to these questions, they will be prepared to answer the only question that really matters: Can the advertising investment be expected to increase profits?

THE BUSINESS OPPORTUNITY

The business opportunity offered by the U.S. Hispanic market can be put in perspective by looking at the role that Hispanic sales play in total annual sales. As a case in point, let us examine what the Hispanic market means to product brand XYZ's total annual sales of $100 million.

The U.S. Hispanic population stands at 15 million, with an additional undocumented alien population estimated at 6 to 8 million, for a total of 21 to 23 million Hispanics. The total United States population is 226 million, with Hispanics representing approximately 10 percent of the total.

For the sake of simplicity, the assumption is made, in this case, that Hispanics and non-Hispanics have the same product-brand consumption levels. It then follows that Hispanics represent 10 percent of total national sales, or $10 million of product brand XYZ's total sales volume.

Now suppose that the product-brand consumption level in the Hispanic market increased by 50 percent as a result of a well-executed national Hispanic advertising campaign. Sales volume in the Hispanic market would rise to $15 million, thereby raising the total national sales to $105 million. The 50 percent increase in Hispanic product-brand consumption level would result in a 5 percent increase in total national sales volume.

Product brand XYZ

Before Hispanic advertising:	
Hispanic sales	$ 10,000,000
National sales	100,000,000
After Hispanic advertising:	
Hispanic sales (50% increase in product-brand consumption)	15,000,000
Increase in Hispanic sales volume	5,000,000
Total annual sales (5% increase in total product-brand consumption)	$105,000,000

The validity of this theoretical model hinges on Hispanic advertising's ability to generate a 50 percent increase in the Hispanic market. When judged by advertising's effect on the *general* market, an increase of 50 percent in product-brand consumption is totally unrealistic. Such an increase in the *Hispanic* market, however, is not as far-fetched as it appears.

Advertising campaigns designed specifically for the Hispanic market have resulted in 25 percent to 200 percent brand-share increases in the national U.S. Hispanic market. These increases have taken no more than 12 months to develop and have been achieved with national yearly Hispanic advertising budgets of less than $1 million.

This does not mean that every product brand entering the Hispanic market nationally has experienced such large increases, but given a well-executed campaign, adequate distribution, and a Hispanic product consumption level comparable with that of the general market, advertisers can expect significant sales increases.

Actual test market results attest to the potential impact of an advertising campaign in the Hispanic market. Brand names are not revealed here owing to the proprietary nature of the information.

| Product | Yearly Hispanic advertising budget | Percent using brand most often | | Percent change | Time period (mo) |
		Before advertising	After advertising		
Brand A— health and beauty aid	$1,000,000	19	38	+100	12
Brand B— food	$800,000	14	18	+ 28	3
Brand C— health and beauty aid	$600,000	2	6	+200	6
Brand D— food	$1,000,000	40	47	+ 17	2
Brand E— food	$800,000	32	51	+ 59	4

A primary reason behind Hispanic advertising's ability to generate such surprising brand-share increases is that the Hispanic market is still underdeveloped. An advertising campaign created specifically for Hispanics remains the exception. Consequently, competition for the Hispanic consumer's attention among brands offering similar products is nowhere as intense as it is in the general market. Because of this lack of competing advertising messages in a particular product category, a Hispanic advertisement has much more impact on its target audience than a general-market commercial has on its target audience.

For a limited investment, an advertiser can currently dominate the Hispanic market share of voice in a single product category to a degree that is simply not possible in the general market at any cost. In tandem with proper creative strategy and supportive research, share-of-voice domination results in quantum increases of 25 to 100 percent in Hispanic brand share within as short a time as 3 to 12 months after the campaign begins.

Imagine for a moment what the brand-share increases would be in the general market if seven out of every ten commercials that the audience heard on the radio or saw on television for a specific product category advertised a single product brand. Imagine that this situation persisted for 6 months or 12 months. Would not brand-share increases of 25 to 100 percent and higher result under these circumstances?

Realistically, this is impossible in the general market, but the advertiser does have the opportunity to enjoy this situation with the 10 percent of the total market that the Hispanic population represents.

CHOOSING THE AGENCY

Should you, as a potential advertiser, decide to enter the Hispanic market, choosing the correct advertising agency to handle the account is one of the first important decisions that you will face. Since you may be as unfamiliar with Hispanic advertising agencies as you are with the Hispanic market, consult as many reliable and knowledgeable sources as are available before choosing the agency.

Talk with other advertisers in the Hispanic market about their experiences with agencies. Read some of the Hispanic marketing or Hispanic advertising articles that appear in the trade magazines. Get opinions from people whose judgment you value.

Once a candidate list has been compiled, look at each agency's history and track record in Hispanic advertising. How long has it been in business? What accounts does it handle? How have these accounts done in the Hispanic market?

Become familiar with the agency's capabilities and philosophy. What does the agency offer in the way of resources, offices, and in-house facilities? What services can the agency provide and not provide? Is the agency essentially a regional or a national agency? Will it work through the general-market agency or directly with the client? What kinds of advertising disciplines and techniques will be applied to the development of the campaign?

Get to know the personnel. What were the key agency personnel doing prior to their present positions? What is the personnel mix, i.e., Hispanic/non-Hispanic/Spanish-origin composition? What skills does each bring to his or her position?

Finally, once you have listened to all relevant opinions, gathered the necessary information, and witnessed the agencies' presentations, make your own decision. The advertiser is the only person in a position to determine his or her requirements in Hispanic advertising and to choose the agency that will best meet those needs. Should the advertiser decide that a Hispanic advertising consultant would be more appropriate than an agency, the same basic considerations used in choosing the agency still apply.

There are a number of advertising agencies with the capability and the expertise to successfully guide and advise the advertiser as to the best course to take in the U.S. Hispanic market. Advertising agencies with Hispanic capability range from (1) independent Hispanic advertising agencies whose total billings are derived strictly from Hispanic advertising to (2) advertising agencies that have significant Hispanic and non-Hispanic representation in their key personnel and/or billings to (3) essentially general-market agencies that offer Hispanic advertising services through a Hispanic division or Hispanic personnel.

Hispanic advertising agencies are a response to marketplace forces. As advertisers became aware of the Hispanic market and began to make special efforts to reach it, they found that general-market agencies had neither the expertise nor the interest in the Hispanic market necessary to develop and implement effective Hispanic advertising. The only ones that had those skills and the interest were the Hispanic advertising agencies. Indeed, the Hispanic agencies were among the first to recognize the true opportunities offered by the U.S. Hispanic market and to stimulate advertiser interest, some as far back as 20 years ago and more.

As the Hispanic market and Spanish media gained in recognition and perceived importance, the number of Hispanic advertising agencies also grew, and there was a new development—general-market agencies began either to create Hispanic advertising divisions or to acquire Hispanic advertising agencies through mergers. To some industry observers, the advent of the Hispanic division was seen as a defensive move by the large general-market agencies who did not want to see any portion of their clients' advertising budgets diverted outside the agency itself to independent Hispanic advertising agencies. To other industry observers, the coming of the Hispanic divisions was seen as a clear indication that Hispanic advertising had arrived and was demanding substantial budgets; otherwise, the "big boys" would have remained uninterested.

Both observations are valid. While mass-audience advertising is and will continue to be the overriding priority for the large general-market agencies, Hispanic advertising interest and billings have grown to the point where the large agencies do not want their clients to go elsewhere for those services. They have therefore taken steps to prevent the Hispanic advertising portion of their clients' overall advertising budgets from going outside the agency, particularly since Hispanic advertising budgets should continue to grow rapidly in the future.

There are different institutional dynamics at work within an independent Hispanic advertising agency than there are within a Hispanic division of a large general-market agency. For an independent agency, Hispanic advertising is its only priority, its livelihood. If it regularly fails at Hispanic advertising, the agency will soon be out of business.

For a Hispanic division within a large general-market agency, Hispanic advertising is also the first priority. Hispanic advertising, however, is not the livelihood of the large general-market agency. If the division fails at Hispanic advertising, it is of relatively small financial consequence to the agency itself. The institutional interests of the large general-market agency may be well-served merely in that the Hispanic division prevents the Hispanic advertising budgets of general-market clients from leaving the agency.

Presenting Hispanic advertising to their clients as a sound business opportunity is of much less importance to the large general-market agency than it is to the small independent Hispanic agency. The economic survival of the Hispanic division is dependent on the financial success of the large agency's general-market efforts, not the other way around. Certainly, the institutional channeling of personnel, technical, and budgetary resources will favor the general-market divisions over the Hispanic divisions as a matter of policy. From the corporate point of view, it only makes good business sense.

On the other hand, the large general-market agency will generally have much greater technical and budgetary resources at its command than the independent Hispanic agency to develop the best possible campaign. This is assuming that the Hispanic division of the large agency will have ready access to these resources.

At the personal level, the differences in dynamics between the independent Hispanic agency and the Hispanic division are diminished. Other factors being equal, the creative director and the account executive at the Hispanic division are just as concerned with doing their jobs and doing them well as their counterparts at the independent Hispanic agency. The personal employee rewards in terms of satisfaction, money, and job security are more or less comparable.

When the same agency is handling both general-market and Hispanic advertising for a product, communication and, potentially, coordination of efforts between the general-market and the Hispanic account groups are facilitated. The degree of communication necessary between the two account groups, however, is small.

From the point of view of the general-market account group, there is very little reason for it to be at all concerned with the Hispanic market implications of the general campaign. The general-market account group will base its decisions on what will work in the general market, period.

The Hispanic advertising group, on the other hand, should be familiar with the product's advertising history in the general market as well as its plans for the future, but there is generally little need to go beyond that. The independent Hispanic agency should encounter little difficulty in acquiring this type of information, although a Hispanic division will naturally have greater access.

In choosing the agency, the advertiser should not eliminate either Hispanic divisions or independent Hispanic agencies from consideration at the outset. As long as the advertisers are aware of the dynamics at play, they will be prepared to make a sound decision.

Whether the advertising is developed and implemented by an independent Hispanic agency or by a Hispanic division may have very little to do with the success of the campaign. It is the quality and professionalism of the individuals who run the campaign and the resources at their command that will determine the success of a Hispanic advertising campaign.

THE TEST MARKET

When the evidence indicates that an advertising investment in the Hispanic market should prove to be profitable, the advertiser will most likely want to try out the advertising campaign in a test market before deciding whether to go national or to expand efforts.

The use of a test market minimizes the initial advertising investment in determining the viability of the Hispanic market. Test market measurements provide advertisers with their first on-the-field data. When properly monitored, the measurements clearly determine the effects that a specific campaign will have on an individual product brand in the Hispanic market. Should the measurements prove positive, the advertiser can then expand his or her efforts with a high degree of confidence in the expected end result. Should the measurements prove disappointing, the advertiser has invested a minimal amount.

Once the advertiser decides to go into a test market, he or she has to be willing to commit the necessary budget to provide a true test of the campaign's effectiveness.

Proper attention should be paid to the development of the test market's creative strategy since the same strategy will very likely be used should the campaign roll out. Since the advertiser is addressing a new market, the campaign should go in with introductory levels of advertising frequency and run for no less than 6 months.

Brand share, awareness, and perception must be determined prior to the implementation of the campaign in order to establish baseline standards for later comparison in determining campaign effectiveness. It is not entirely necessary to wait until these data are in, however, before beginning to develop the campaign.

Postcampaign attitudinal and usage studies must also be an integral part of the test market budget. Monitoring instruments for measuring product movement levels in the test market should be implemented whenever possible. Advertising recall tests should also be considered. Throughout the test market experience, the advertiser should keep in mind that one of the test market's primary purposes is to determine the campaign's effect.

Following is a series of brief case histories from actual test market experiences for a variety of product categories. Proprietary limitations prevent the disclosure of brand names.

Brand A—Health and Beauty Aid Product   Brand A began its Hispanic advertising test in March 1978 with Spanish television as the only variable. Brand A's share of the market was 19 percent among Hispanics and required a share increase of 4 points, to 23 percent, in order for the Hispanic advertising to pay off.

Location: southwest United States (75 percent of total market)

Duration: 6 to 12 months

Measurements: pre- and postusage studies, special Nielsen panels, SAMI (Selling Areas Marketing, Inc.) area shipments

Budget: working media, $50,000 to $100,000; production (two 30-second commercials, $50,000; total, $100,000 to $150,000

After 6 months of advertising, brand A's share of the market had exceeded the 23 percent objective and reached 26 percent. After 12 months, brand A's market share had climbed to 38 percent, a 100 percent increase in brand share within the Hispanic market.

	Before advertising	After 6 months of advertising	After 12 months of advertising
Brand used most often*	19%	26%	38%

*Combined test markets.

SAMI data confirmed Hispanic advertising's effectiveness by tracking increases in product movement.

SAMI Test Market Increase vs. U.S. Total

	Percent change	
	Test market I	Test market II
Dollar share	+22	+ 60
Package share	+46	+123

While brand A's share in the market was climbing to the 50 percent level in Spanish television markets carrying advertising, its share remained depressed in Spanish radio markets, in which it was not carrying on a Hispanic advertising campaign.

Brand Share in Spanish Radio Market without Advertising Campaign: November 1979

Unaided awareness at first mention	16.1%
Brand used most often	20.9%
Brand bought last	21.8%

A subsequent radio test in a market without Spanish television documented the ability of Hispanic advertising on Spanish radio to generate dramatic sales increases.

	Before advertising (%)	After advertising (%)	Percent change
Brand awareness:			
Aided	81	97	+ 20
Unaided	16	37	+131
Brand used most often	21	38	+ 80

Brand B—Food   In November 1979, brand B initiated a Hispanic advertsing test using Spanish television as the only medium. The test required a 12 percent increase in shipments to the test area in order for the advertising investment to pay off.

After the 13 weeks of advertising, shipments to the test area were up 29 percent relative to the control area, well above the 12 percent increase necessary for payoff.

	Base, 10/21/78–10/20/79	Cumulative, 10/21/79–2/8/80
Test shipments	751	1013
Percent change relative to previous year	−6.0	+44.3
Cumulative/base ratio (%)	—	135
Test market/control area ratio (%)	—	+29

Brand awareness and purchase indices had also risen sharply after 13 weeks of advertising.

	Before advertising (%)	After advertising (%)	Percent change
Brand awareness:			
Aided	73	91*	+24
Unaided	42	63*	+50
Advertising awareness:			
Aided	49	74*	+50
Unaided	15	40*	+166
Ever bought:			
Aided	48	56*	+16
Unaided	32	41*	+28
Bought past month	14	20*	+42
Buy most often	14	18	+28
Buy next time	41	47	+14

* 95% confidence level.

Brand C—Health and Beauty Aid In 1979 and 1980, brand C conducted a Hispanic advertising test in San Antonio. The brand required a 3.1 share point increase in the test area relative to the control area in order for the Hispanic advertising to pay off.

	Share of market (share points)			Change relative to base (share points)	Test market growth increment (share points)
	Base period, Nov./Dec. 1978–Mar./ Apr. 1979	Test period, May/June 1979–Nov./ Dec. 1979	Latest, Nov./Dec. 1979		
San Antonio total market (test)	21.9	25.7	28.3	+6.4	
Remainder of border district (control)	25.8	26.5	28.0	+2.2	+4.2
Remainder of United States (control)	27.0	28.0	28.9	+1.9	+4.5

After 8 months of advertising, brand C's share of the test market had increased 4.2 share points relative to the control area, as compared with the 3.1 share point objective. Results were measured by a special Nielsen Hispanic store panel.

By comparison, in 1977 and 1978, brand C had increased its advertising levels on English language media for a test in San Antonio. The test had no effect on business. Sales actually went down 3 percent in the test area as compared with control areas.

Brand D—Food Significant brand increases in the Hispanic test market due to Spanish advertising are often discernible after as little as 2 months from the beginning of a campaign. In 1979, brand D ran a campaign using Los Angeles as a Hispanic test market. After only 8 weeks of advertising, the following increases were measured among Los Angeles Hispanic households:

	Before advertising (%)	After advertising (%)	Percent change
Unaided awareness:			
Brand	79	89	+12
Advertising	25	37	+48
Used in past 3 months	54	64	+18
Buy most often	40	47	+17
Have on hand	39	48	+23

Brand E—Food It would not be fair, however, to make a final judgment on Hispanic market reaction to Spanish advertising based on only 2 months of advertising experience. The effect of advertising on product movement and brand awareness should be allowed sufficient time to develop in order to be measured most accurately. After 6 months of Hispanic advertising in Los Angeles, the well-established brand E had conclusive results.

	Before advertising (%)	After advertising (%)	Percent change
Market share*	60	73	+22
Used in past 3 months	43	60	+40
Buy most often	32	51	+59
Have on hand	32	43	+34

* Over a 6-month test period.

The Test Market Site

The choice of test markets is very important and depends to a large extent on the advertiser's plans should the test market experience prove successful. The makeup of the Hispanic population in the test market should reflect the intended Hispanic audience were the campaign to roll out.

For good reasons, two of the most popular Hispanic test markets are San Antonio and Chicago. Both cities offer five Spanish radio stations each, as well as a television station. Neither city has a daily Spanish newspaper, but owing to the Hispanic market's heavy orientation toward the broadcast media, this is of little importance. Weekly Spanish publications are available.

San Antonio represents one of the most well established Hispanic communities in the United States. The San Antonio ADI is the third-largest Hispanic market in the United States, with a population of 849,000 Hispanics as of January 1980. The San Antonio Hispanic population is over 95 percent Mexican according to the U.S. Census Bureau.

Because of its heavy Mexican population, San Antonio is a favorite test site for advertisers primarily interested in the Mexican-origin population. Moreover, since Mexicans represent 59 percent of the national U.S. Hispanic population, San Antonio is also very popular for Hispanic campaigns that intend to go nationwide. Tracking of product movement and monitoring of attitudinal and usage levels in the San Antonio Hispanic market are greatly facilitated by the fact that its total population is 59 percent Hispanic. This represents another plus for its use as a test market.

Chicago is the sixth-largest Hispanic market in the United States, with a population of 660,100 Hispanics as of January 1980. Its uniqueness as a test site lies in the fact that no Spanish-origin group totally dominates the market. Of all major U.S. Hispanic markets, Chicago's Hispanic composition most closely parallels the national Hispanic population according to Spanish-origin group. The national Hispanic population is 59 percent Mexican, 15 percent Puerto Rican, 6 percent Cuban, and 20 percent other. Chicago's Hispanic population is also primarily Mexican, followed by a substantial Puerto Rican segment. Sizable Cuban and Central and South American segments are also found in the city's Hispanic population. Because of this breakdown of its Spanish-origin groups, the success or failure of a campaign in reaching any of the major Spanish-origin groups can be determined in the field before going national.

There are many other appropriate test sites for Hispanic advertising. In choosing the test site, the advertiser should primarily look at the makeup of the local Hispanic population, the availability of Spanish media, and the potential for accurately measuring the campaign's effectiveness.

CONCLUSION

The advertiser should approach the U.S. Hispanic market as a business opportunity, not as an obligation, nor as an afterthought. For most consumer goods, the Hispanic market offers a combination of low advertising costs and high consumer response that simply does not exist in the general market. Whether Hispanic advertising makes sense for the individual advertiser can be determined with little expense and effort. Trial entry, by way of a test market, entails little financial risk.

Unfamiliarity with the Hispanic market should not in itself dissuade the advertiser from making the decision to enter. The U.S. Hispanic market is actually a relatively easy one to reach and to persuade through the available Spanish media.

Over 50 percent of the Hispanic consumers in the United States are located in six cities; over 30 percent live in either New York or Los Angeles. The one trait that most typifies U.S. Hispanics—Spanish language use—also characterizes the most effective way to reach and persuade them—through Spanish language media.

Moreover, there are experienced and competent professionals in Hispanic advertising who have the necessary skills and understanding to develop and implement marketing and advertising plans that will effectively persuade the Hispanic marketplace.

LISTINGS—HISPANIC ADVERTISING AGENCIES

The following list is alphabetical by state and city. It includes advertising agencies that specialize strictly in Hispanic advertising, Hispanic divisions within major general-market advertising agencies, and small advertising agencies that offer both general and Hispanic advertising services. The list is current as of June 1981.

The list is not exhaustive; it does, however, feature every major national Hispanic advertising agency as well as several smaller and/ or regional advertising agencies that have come to the attention of the authors as suppliers of Hispanic advertising services.

Key to Listings:

First line   Agency or division and affiliation (if division)
Second line   Address
Third line   Telephone number
Fourth line   Key personnel

CALIFORNIA

Los Angeles

Bermudez & Associates
6290 Sunset Blvd., Hollywood, CA 90028
(213) 851-1011
Eduardo Bermudez

Cervera International Corporation
1666 N. McCadden Pl., Hollywood, CA 90028
(213) 464-2346
Ernesto Cervera

Kessler & Eisele Advertising
8322 Beverly Blvd., Los Angeles, CA 90048
(213) 655-6040
Colette Eisele

Newport Beach

Mendoza, Dillon & Asociados
1601 Dove St., Newport Beach, CA 92660
(714) 851-1811
Richard Dillon

Noble & Asociados USA
500 Newport Center Dr., Newport Beach, CA 92660
(714) 644-7223
Ernesto Balleste

San Jose

Inter-American Advertising
5389 Meridian Ave., San Jose, CA 95118
(408) 266-5100
Eduardo H. Grigg Patoni

FLORIDA

Miami

Allan Advertising, Inc.
6360 N.E. 4th Ct., Miami, FL 33138
(305) 751-1181
W. Allan Sandler

Arregui International Advertising
5825 S.W. 8th St., Miami, FL 33144
(305) 264-9500
Ricardo Arregui

International Marketing & Advertising Services
2801 Ponce De Leon Blvd., Coral Gables, FL 33141
(305) 442-9540
Francisco Vergara

Publitec International, Inc.
1110 Brickell Ave., Miami, FL 33131
(305) 371-6274
Isabel Norniella

SAMS of Florida, Inc./D'Arcy-MacManus & Masius Group
250 Catalonia Ave., Coral Gables, FL 33134
(305) 446-5572
Ernesto Cordobes

Zubi Advertising Services, Inc.
2525 S.W. Third Ave., Miami, FL 33129
(305) 854-6807
Teresa Zubizarreta

ILLINOIS

Chicago

Jorge Caballero & Assoc.
410 S. Michigan Ave., Chicago, IL 60605
(312) 939-1410
Jorge Caballero

Lesmes Productions, Inc.
8039 W. Leyland Ave., Norwidge, IL 60656
(312) 456-1512
Louis Lesmes

March Advertising
4432 N. Richmond, Chicago, IL 60625
(312) 463-7835
Jesse Wilson

OMAR
5525 N. Broadway, Chicago, IL 60640
(312) 371-1686
Marcelino Miyares

RJP Advertising, Inc.
868 N. Wabash, Chicago, IL 60611
(312) 642-7935
Richard J. Paredes

San José & Associates
327 S. La Salle St., Chicago, IL 60604
(312) 663-5620
George San José

Skokie

Miranda Advertising Corporation
3719 Enfield, Skokie, IL 60076
(312) 674-0060
Orlando Miranda

NEW JERSEY

Secaucus

Interamericas Advertising
100 Seaview Dr., Secaucus, NJ 07094
(201) 348-8331
Justo Rodriguez

Union City

Hudson Advertising
3229 Bergenline Ave., Union City, NJ 07087
(201) 864-2111
Rafael De Olive

NEW MEXICO

Santa Fe

Delgado Advertising
P.O. Box 1906, Santa Fe, NM 87501
(505) 982-4659
Ed Delgado

NEW YORK

New York

Access Advertising & Marketing, Inc.
45 E. 51st St., New York, NY 10022
(212) 759-5488
Lou Cabrera

Adelante Advertising, Inc.
588 Fifth Ave., New York, NY 10036
(212) 869-1470
Sy Davis

The Bravo Group/Young & Rubicam, Inc.
285 Madison Ave., New York, NY 10017
(212) 953-2000
Jim Murtagh

Conill Advertising Assoc., Inc.
501 Fifth Ave., New York, NY 10017
(212) 661-6588
Alicia Conill

CSI International
545 Fifth Ave., New York, NY 10017
(212) 867-4065
Castor Fernandez

Diaz-Albertini Enterprises
300 E. 54th St., New York, NY 10022
(212) 888-0468
Luis Diaz-Albertini

Hispania/J. Walter Thompson
420 Lexington Ave., New York, NY 10017
(212) 867-3910
Antonio Ruiz

Hispano-American Adv.
230 Park Ave., New York, NY 10017
(212) 697-6313
Ralph Infante

JonRob Advertising, Inc.
271 Madison Ave., New York, NY 10016
(212) 354-9000
Robert Resnik

Merosa Advertising
200 W. 57th St., New York, NY 10019
(212) 246-7565
Salvador Merced

Nu-Line Advertising Agency
200 W. 58th St., New York, NY 10017
(212) 265-0727
Anibal Gonzalez

D. L. Passante Associates, Inc.
1619 Broadway, New York, NY 10019
(212) 265-0220
Don L. Passante

Publicidad Siboney
919 Third Ave., New York, NY 10022
(212) 751-9985
Alex Berger

SAMS, Inc./D'Arcy-MacManus & Masius Group
605 Third Ave., New York, NY 10016
(212) 682-5000
David Newman

T.D.A. Advertising
30 E. 42d St., New York, NY 10017
(212) 687-1433
Antonio Diaz-Albertini

Uniworld Group
1250 Broadway, New York, NY 10001
(212) 564-0066
Bryon Lewis

TEXAS

Corpus Christi

Maya Advertising, Inc.
4455 S. Padre Island Dr., Corpus Christi, TX 78411
(512) 855-4836
Rex W. Eagon

San Antonio

Atkins Advertising
1802 N.E. Loop 410, San Antonio, TX 78217
(512) 828-0611
Felipe Cantu

Sosa & Associates
One Romana Plaza, San Antonio, TX 78205
(512) 227-2013
Lionel Sosa

Chapter 9

Creative Strategy

The departure point in the development of a successful creative strategy specifically for U.S. Hispanics is the recognition that one is addressing a new market. The creative strategy that has proven successful in the general market will not necessarily enjoy the same degree of success in the Hispanic market. It *might* prove to be successful, but advertisers should not enter the market with their minds set on using the same strategy. Instead, they should begin the process of determining the most effective approach to follow by applying the same disciplines in the Hispanic market that are applied in the general market.

Make use of focus groups, mass surveys, and other research tools to gather necessary information upon which to base creative strategy. Ask the Hispanic market the same series of questions concerning product-brand perception that is asked of the general market, for example. Test the copy, and run commercial recall tests upon reaching the appropriate stage in campaign development.

There is no reason to develop creative strategy in a void when research can provide reliable information that will greatly facilitate decision making. Not only will such research ensure that the creative strategy is headed in the right direction, it will also lift the mist of unfamiliarity that envelops the U.S. Hispanic market for so many advertisers.

U.S. Hispanics and non-Hispanics have vastly different lifestyles. Consequently, developing a creative strategy that will trigger the desired response must be approached from a different perspective. To achieve the desired response, the advertising stimuli must be based on a perception of the world as seen through the eyes of the U.S. Hispanic. This perception is shaped by three determining cultural characteristics: prevalent use of the Spanish language, close family ties, and strong adherence to Roman Catholicism. Advertising that ignores these three attributes will have little, if any, positive impact on U.S. Hispanics. Conversely, advertising that avails itself of these three concepts is well on its way toward a successful campaign.

LANGUAGE

The most universal and culturally unifying characteristic of U.S. Hispanics is their use of Spanish, either as a primary or as a secondary language. The same language is used by every one of the twenty Spanish-speaking nationalities comprising the U.S. Hispanic population. However, there are nationality colorations related to pronunciation, cadence, and the meaning of individual words, just as there are colorations among English speakers.

The use of the Spanish language is not limited to older Hispanics, as is sometimes believed. According to a study conducted by the U.S. Department of Commerce in July 1976, over 64 percent of the Spanish-origin population under 20 years of age prefers its native tongue. The same study showed that over 50 percent of the Spanish-origin population with college education has retained use of the Spanish language. Over 65 percent of the people who identified themselves in the study as being of Spanish origin lived in households where Spanish was usually spoken. More recent estimates place the use of Spanish in the homes of the U.S. Spanish-origin population at 80 percent or more.

The recently released Yankelovich study, *Spanish USA*, conducted in 1981 for SIN, found that 99 percent of the study's self-identified "Hispanic descent or background" respondents spoke at least "enough Spanish to get by." Of the Hispanic-descent respondents, 90 percent spoke Spanish fluently or as a primary language, 47 percent were bilingual, and 23 percent knew Spanish only. Only 1 percent of the Hispanic-descent respondents knew English only.

The enduring power of Spanish language use by the U.S. Hispanic population has been partly due to the constant replenishment it receives from the large numbers of yearly Hispanic immigrants to the United States as well as to modern communications and transportation, which help to keep ties to Spanish-speaking countries of origin alive and strong. The relatively recent development in American society of maintaining and expressing pride in ethnic heritage has also played its part. The enduring power of Spanish language use by U.S. Hispanics is perhaps most attributable, however, to its direct and positive connection with the family and the home.

When a Hispanic child is born in the United States, the first words he or she hears will likely be in Spanish. During the first few years of life, the child will be in daily contact with the Spanish language, if only in the home environment. More than likely the home will also be located in an area populated by other Spanish-speaking families who will shape many of the child's first contacts. The Hispanic child will most likely also be in daily contact with the English language. Ideally, capability in both languages will develop equally, although this is seldom the case.

Once the child reaches school age, proficiency in the English language begins to develop quickly. Initially it will be disconcerting for the child to be in a formal school environment that constantly demands facility in the English language; nevertheless, English competency usually develops quickly.

Because of the Spanish language's close association with the home and the family, the child develops a positive attitude early in life toward speaking Spanish, an attitude that is usually retained. Since the use of Spanish outside of the home may be discouraged by the dominant English-speaking society, this positive reinforcement is all the more important.

For the Hispanic who comes to the United States as an adult, a different process influences Spanish and English language use. Most Hispanics who immigrate to the United States are initially drawn to areas with high Hispanic concentrations by the magnet of a familiar language and culture. Within a Hispanic enclave, the newly arrived immigrants can function on a day-to-day basis without experiencing a pressing need to learn English instantly. They can find out where to live, shop, and possibly work without being forced to venture very far outside of the Hispanic enclave. Just as importantly, within the Hispanic pocket, the recent immigrants feel a sense of belonging that they would not enjoy in a predominantly English-speaking environment.

Living in a primarily Spanish-speaking environment is both functionally and psychologically important to the recent Hispanic immigrant. However, competing forces draw the Hispanic outside of a primarily Spanish-speaking environment.

While job opportunities exist within the Hispanic enclave, more jobs, as well as better-quality employment, are available outside the Hispanic enclave, even for those with limited English-speaking ability. Since economic improvement is one of the prime motivations for immigrating to the United States, better job opportunities provide a strong incentive to leave the Hispanic enclave, be it for a few hours every day, for a number of consecutive days, weeks, or months, or for permanent residence. Housing opportunities provide the same type of inducement as do educational opportunities, particularly for the young Hispanic.

Living within or outside of the Hispanic enclave, however, does not provide an either/or choice in terms of living in a Spanish or English monolingual environment. Regardless of place of residence, the U.S. Hispanic will encounter the English language on a more or less daily basis and will develop some English language proficiency. The degree of English language and Spanish language proficiency will largely rest on where the Hispanic lives, works, shops, goes to school, and spends leisure time. For U.S. Hispanics, many of these activities occur within a primarily Spanish-speaking environment.

There is no reason to believe that U.S. Hispanics will abandon the widespread use of the Spanish language. On the contrary, past history and current evidence point to retention of Spanish as a primary or secondary language, particularly in verbal communication. Spanish language use will retain its positive association as a direct psychological tie to the family. The Spanish-speaking environment will continue to provide the U.S. Hispanic with a sense of identity and belonging.

Spanish language use is such an integral part of the Hispanic culture that one is inseparable from the other. For U.S. Hispanics, surrendering Spanish language use would be tantamount to surrendering a vital part of their identity, something they have no intention of doing.

FAMILY TIES

At a time when traditional American family values are under the greatest stress, the U.S. Hispanic family is an exception. It is characterized by strong and close bonds that frequently extend outside the nuclear family to include grandparents, aunts, uncles, cousins, and non-family members who are treated as family by virtue of long-standing associations.

In the U.S. Hispanic home, it is not unusual to find three generations living together or to find an aunt or an uncle living with the nuclear family. Owing to strong family bonds, it is also not unusual to find a son or daughter living at home past the time when an American child would generally have established a separate household.

Close ties to the family are not lost when the Hispanic establishes a separate household, be it because of marriage, employment, or some other reason. Family members added through marriage are made to feel that they belong, that they are an integral part of the family. Contact with the family remains frequent, and efforts are made to get together, particularly for holidays and other special occasions.

From childhood and throughout their adult lives, U.S. Hispanics retain close family ties. Even during the teenage years, when the child's peer group becomes increasingly important and vies for influence with the family in shaping the child's personal identity, the Hispanic teenager remains close to the family. It is primarily during this time that Hispanic youngsters work out in their minds what it means to be Hispanic in a dominant American society. The teenage years generally are also the time during which the Hispanic is most open to internalizing influences outside the family, adopting American cultural values and behavior that are retained in later years.

The family plays a primary role in the transmission of Hispanic cultural and social values. The role that the U.S. Hispanic family plays in this respect is particularly important in that the dominant American society promotes divergent, at times conflicting, cultural and social values. In fact, its place within the dominant American society requires that the U.S. Hispanic family fulfill cutural transmission functions that are normally fulfilled by larger institutions and other influences when the family culture and the dominant culture are the same. The role played by the U.S. Hispanic family in the maintenance of the Spanish language is an integral part of the family's cultural transmission function.

For the U.S. Hispanic, the interplay between the family, the Hispanic culture, and the Spanish language is mutually supportive. The close bonds of the U.S. Hispanic family enhance its ability to transmit Hispanic cultural and social values and to maintain the Spanish language. Similarly, use of the Spanish language and adherence to Hispanic cultural and social values within the framework of a different dominant culture serve to remind the Hispanic of the family and to nourish family ties.

THE CATHOLIC RELIGION

Approximately 85 percent of the U.S. Hispanic population is Roman Catholic, giving the Catholic religion a tremendous influence in the value system and lifestyle of U.S. Hispanics. This influence notwithstanding, strict adherence to church teachings and to religious beliefs and practices varies. Religious observance revolves around the family and finds its deepest expression among women.

The Roman Catholic influence is clearly evident in the Hispanic family's close ties and respect for elders. The Catholic church's influence is demographically demonstrated by the Hispanic family's larger size, due in part to the church's prohibition of practicing birth control. It is also evident in the lower divorce rate of Hispanics as compared with that of the general population.

The charitable nature of U.S. Hispanics and their willingness to help other people and share what they have are also partly founded in the concept of brotherhood and of helping the unfortunate as espoused by the Catholic faith. An appeal for funds or assistance to help victims of a disaster or to aid the needy rarely goes unanswered in the U.S. Hispanic community. This charity and willingness to give are directed toward people rather than toward social institutions. The person-to-person style and connection are essential. U.S. Hispanics will give to a person many times before giving to an institution.

In a larger sense, the Catholic church inculcates Hispanics with a deep appreciation for spiritual and humanistic values. Certainly, U.S. Hispanics are interested in material possessions and will work long and hard to achieve material goals; economic improvement is the primary reason why most Hispanics come to the United States. However, the Hispanic has a concurrent appreciation for the nonmaterial things in life and attempts to strike a balance.

Throughout its history the Catholic church has been a most-respected and trusted institution by U.S. Hispanics. Indeed, one of the driving forces behind the exploration and colonization undertaken by Spain was the establishment of the Catholic church in the new world and the spreading of the Catholic faith. Today in many parishes and in many cities, Hispanics represent the majority of practicing Catholics. The long-standing Catholic tradition in the Hispanic culture and the high status currently enjoyed by the Catholic church ensure that Catholicism will continue to play an influential part in the value system and lifestyle of U.S. Hispanics.

ATTITUDINAL SIMILARITIES

While Spanish language use, close family ties, and adherence to Roman Catholicism are at the heart of the U.S. Hispanic's cultural identity, other lifestyle similarities are also evident. Attitudinal characteristics play a determining role in shaping the U.S. Hispanic lifestyle and have direct application in the development of an effective creative strategy for anyone seeking to influence the Hispanic market.

Food   Whether at home or at a restaurant, food is to be enjoyed; the number of calories or the cholesterol level is of little interest. The nutritional value of food does gain importance when it is to be served to children. The types of preferred food vary across nationality lines; however, the taste remains the most important quality of food for all Hispanics.

Music Hispanics have an emotional affinity toward music and dancing that can be put to good use in the communication of a commercial message. While musical preferences differ according to nationality and region, there are styles that cut across these lines, touching all Hispanic groups.

Leisure Time Leisure time is highly valued by U.S. Hispanics and centers around the family and close friends. When it is time to relax and enjoy, matters relating to the job are left behind. The important thing is to share a good time with family and friends.

Loyalty Once personal trust is won, the Hispanic tends to remain loyal. In brand preference, this means that conclusive evidence of superiority is necessary before the Hispanic will switch brands. Direct faultfinding attacks on a favorite brand, however, might backfire. A better approach would be to emphasize strong points of an advertised brand without knocking competing brands.

Pride Hispanics are very proud of their heritage and will deeply resent negative stereotyping in commercials. Placing a Hispanic character in a helpless position in a commercial will also create ill feelings, as will poking fun at Hispanic traits or individuals.

Quality Product quality is of great importance to Hispanics. Within affordable limits, they want the best for their family and for themselves. An economy approach will be effective only if the brand has established a reputation for quality; economy by itself will seldom sell a product to Hispanics.

Recognition The Hispanic wants to be recognized as a productive and integral member of American society. While Hispanics resist assimilation, they are not separatists. They want to remain Hispanic within American society, not outside of it. Ties to homeland, however, remain strong and are not perceived as conflicting with ties to American society.

Tradition Hispanics respect and are great believers in tradition. This appreciation applies to cultural tradition, family tradition, and the tradition of a product or brand. Long-established products could well use this appreciation in their advertising campaign.

Work Ethic Hispanics place great import on meeting their job-related responsibilities and on advancing through hard work. Economic opportunities brought most Hispanics to the United States. The Hispanic, however, is not a workaholic and will not place job obligations above family responsibilities.

CHARACTER PORTRAYAL

The people that appear in an advertisement are an integral element in the development of an environment that is culturally pleasing to the Hispanic. The characters should be recognizably Hispanic without going to the extreme of being one-dimensional stereotypes. By the same token, an advertisement peopled only by characters that are obviously non-Hispanic will greatly diminish the campaign's persuasive power with the Hispanic audience.

In presenting a home setting, advertisers should be aware that the extended family is common. Situations that exemplify the closeness of the family or that bring family members close together can be very effective. An advertisement for a food product that shows the mother teaching a child a family recipe and then serving the finished dish at the table is a good example.

In line with conservative Hispanic values, advertisements should stress the importance of harmony within the family. Advertisements that bring about a reconciliation among family members as a result of product use would be well-received.

The U.S. Hispanic family is male-centered; however, this male orientation should not be viewed in simplistic machismo terms. It is not simply a case of "the husband rules and the wife obeys," as is more prevalent in Latin American countries. Major decisions affecting the family are generally discussed by all adult family members, with adult female family members usually playing an active role in the decision-making process. Once a decision is reached, however, it is the male head of household who implements and enforces it and to whom the final decision is usually attributed. Once the final decision is made, it is expected that all family members, male and female, will accept and support it.

Male and female roles are clearly defined in the U.S. Hispanic family. The primary responsibility of the Hispanic male head of household is to provide the financial income for his family. For some Hispanics it is undesirable that a female family member work outside of the home. This may be seen as a failure by the male head of the household to provide fully for his family. Nevertheless, U.S. Hispanic female employment is on the rise and has lost some of its negative connotations both for the female and for her male partner.

A positive attitude toward Hispanic males doing "women's work" inside the home has been slower in developing. Household chores essentially remain the domain of the woman. Taking care of the home is regarded as important by the typical U.S. Hispanic woman, and she takes pride and pleasure in being competent as a housewife. She should not be portrayed as one of the harried housewives that occasionally appear in commercials in the United States.

The perception of elders as wise and productive people, together with a deeply felt appreciation for what they have contributed to the family, gives them a special place within the U.S. Hispanic family. Even when the elderly cease to be actively productive and have to be cared for, they are not perceived as a burden any more than a child who has to be cared for is perceived as a burden.

Children in the Hispanic family are usually closely supervised, particularly the girls. Children are taught clear rules as to what is right and wrong and are expected to adhere to them. Direct questioning of parental authority is not tolerated and is quickly disciplined, without an ensuing loss of parental affection. Physical and emotional closeness is both nurtured and imposed.

In character portrayal, advertisers should emphasize the Hispanic woman's traditional role as wife, mother, and homemaker. In another context, Hispanic women should also be portrayed as fashion-conscious and as taking pride in their appearance. The advertiser should, nevertheless, be aware of the fact that portrayals of Hispanic women in nontraditional roles are increasingly gaining acceptance. Male characters should lean toward strong personalities but not be presented as overbearing. They should not be portrayed in positions subordinate to other characters or to circumstances. Elders should be accorded respect, and children should be depicted as treasured, but not as spoiled.

COORDINATION WITH GENERAL CAMPAIGN

Occasionally, general-audience advertising campaigns can be successfully adapted for the Hispanic market. Hispanics, after all, do watch English language television, listen to English radio, and read English print. They are exposed to English language commercials, although not necessarily persuaded by them. If the English commercial delivers essentially the same message as the Spanish commercial, however, it is logical to assume that exposure to the same message in both languages will enhance the campaign's overall persuasive power with Hispanics. More specifically, the English commercials will reinforce the persuasion message of the Spanish commercials. Additionally, it is generally less expensive to adapt an established advertising campaign into Spanish than to develop an independent creative concept.

Building a Hispanic advertising campaign around the general campaign may be a wise decision by the advertiser. Before following this path, however, advertisers must first determine that the general-campaign concept is relevant to Hispanics and that it will persuade them to purchase their products or use their services. The advertiser has to remember that the general-audience campaign has been developed on the basis of a series of decisions as to what is most effective in the general market, not in the Hispanic market. Additionally, advertisers have to recognize not only that there are differences in cultures, lifestyles, and attitudes, but also that they are addressing a new market. Product claims and perceptions that have long become part of the general audience's experience will be unfamiliar to the Hispanic market.

If the general creative concept is not relevant, building the Hispanic campaign around it will largely result in a waste of time and money—resources much better spent in the development of an original Hispanic advertising campaign.

Given that the general concept is persuasive with Hispanics, the advertiser must realize, nevertheless, that it is a creative adaptation that is needed, not a translation.

It is the meaning, not the words, that is important.

For example, the slogan "Have a Pepsi day" loses much of its meaning when translated verbatum into Spanish. The phrase upon which the slogan is based, "Have a nice day," is so ingrained in American speech that the connection between the slogan and the phrase is made subliminally. This is not the case in Spanish. The creative adaptation made by the Hispanic advertising agency was "Que te vaya Pepsi bien," or "May things go Pepsi well with you" (which incidentally does not sound nearly as good when translated verbatim into English as it does in Spanish). It does, however, get across the concept of "Have a Pepsi good day" very effectively in Spanish, which is the intended message of the slogan and which does have meaning for Hispanics.

Adaptation of a general campaign usually entails more than just words. Often, the situation in which the action develops has to be changed to something that is more familiar to the Hispanic, although the communicated meaning remains the same. A commercial that centers on action on snow-covered ski slopes might be much better off centered on action at the beach. A conversation between two spectators at a football game should be moved to a soccer match or a baseball game.

In the case of commercial jingles, not only should the lyrics be adapted but possibly the instrumentation as well. At times, it may be preferable to compose new music altogether while communicating the same commercial message.

Because of the production costs, the advertiser often urges that a television commercial use the same video in its Hispanic adaptation as in the general campaign. More often than not, this is a mistake. No matter how exact the dubbing, Hispanics will not identify with a commercial peopled strictly with non-Hispanic characters mouthing Spanish words. Moreover, the advertiser is subconsciously communicating a reluctance to recognize the worth of the Hispanic audience by not creating a commercial especially for it. It is the difference between getting a new set of clothes and receiving hand-me-downs from an unfamiliar person.

If the commercial features characters that are recognizably Hispanic or if the people on screen play a minor role in the communication of a message, the advertiser may be on more solid ground. Certainly, if the advertisement is devoid of people and if the visual message and the creative concept are in tune with the Hispanic, there is little reason for not using the same video in a creative adaptation.

Usually the general-audience commercials have long been in the can before the decision to shoot a Hispanic adaptation is made. With farsighted planning, however, at least some of the production costs of shooting a Hispanic television commercial can be avoided.

Given that the creative concept and the visual environment are relevant to both the general and the Hispanic market, both types of commercials can be shot one after the other. Once the English commercial is completed, it is a simple matter to bring the Hispanic talent on the set and shoot the adaptation with the same production crew, lighting, etc. Minor adjustments in the set, to give it more of a Hispanic flavor, can be easily handled. To ensure that the Hispanic commercial is shot as conceptualized, it would be wise to bring in a Hispanic director or a creative consultant for the shooting who is thoroughly familiar with the adaptation.

NATIONAL VERSUS REGIONAL APPROACH

Shortly after making the entry into the U.S. Hispanic market, the advertiser is inevitably faced with the question of either producing a national campaign that will address the Hispanic market across Spanish-origin lines or producing a campaign that will address Spanish-origin groups individually according to their regional concentrations. The controversy centers on Spanish language use according to national origin, with music preferences and food-preparation differences as secondary considerations.

The line of thinking for the national approach essentially argues that Spanish language use is the most universal and culturally unifying characteristic of U.S. Hispanics, that a generic Spanish language should be used in advertising, and that this neutral Spanish will effectively persuade all Spanish-speaking nationalities. This generic, or broadcast, Spanish is likened to the broadcast English used by reporters and anchors in the national network news programs.

National-approach proponents argue that differences in Spanish language use according to region parallel differences in English language use according to region in the United States. Southern Americans do not speak English in the same manner as Boston Americans or Texans or west coast Americans. Each area has its regionalisms, yet they all speak the same English language. General-market advertising does not emphasize these differences; rather, it is devoid of regionalisms. In Spanish advertising, the same philosophy should be followed, they argue.

Proponents of the regional approach argue that regional differences in Spanish language use are much more extreme than those that exist in English language use within the United States. They say that differences in use of the Spanish language are more like the differences in use of the English language between the United States, Australia, Canada, and Great Britain. All four countries speak English, but the differences in pronunciation, cadence, and meaning of specific words are so extreme that different speaking styles must be used in an advertising situation. Certainly, they all understand what is said in a neutral English, but an advertising message in neutral English is not nearly as persuasive as it would be in a more characteristic speaking style.

The regional approach argues that the decision to advertise in Spanish is made because advertisers believe that a Spanish language campaign brings them closer to the Hispanic consumer than an English language campaign does. It then follows that advertisers should use the Spanish style that brings them closest to the Hispanic population in the specific market that they are trying to persuade.

Both the national and the regional approach follow logical lines of reasoning but are based on different premises. The regional approach says that regional differences in Spanish language use within the U.S. Hispanic market are wide enough to warrant the use of different Spanish styles in advertising; the national approach says that they are not. In theory, one is right and the other wrong. In practice, both approaches have proved successful. The approach that is best-suited for the individual advertiser depends on the target audience, the available media, and the advertising budget.

If primarily interested in reaching one of the three major Spanish-origin groups—Mexicans, Puerto Ricans, and Cubans—the advertising should develop the creative strategy around those qualities that specifically define that one Spanish-origin group. This entails the use not only of a characteristic Spanish style, but also of music, food, settings, and situations typical to that one Spanish-origin group.

For example, if the advertiser is only interested in the San Antonio Hispanic market, it makes sense to give a Mexican flavor to the advertising; San Antonio's Hispanic population is over 95 percent Mexican. If the advertiser is interested in a pluralistic Hispanic market such as Chicago, however, the advertiser should make use of the common denominators in the Hispanic population and use a generic approach in language style and all other elements of the creative strategy.

At the national level, the advertiser can develop extremely effective campaigns that will be persuasive with all Spanish-origin groups by concentrating on qualities common to all Hispanics and by staying away from those that are particular to a single Hispanic group. In other words, a generic campaign should emphasize the similarities and avoid the differences in the U.S. Hispanic market.

In developing a national Hispanic campaign, the advertiser should be very conscious of the Spanish language style: enunciation, rhythm of delivery, and the accepted usage of specific words by all Spanish-origin groups. The script should be reviewed by members of at least the three major U.S. Hispanic-origin groups—Mexican, Puerto Rican, and Cuban—to ensure that the wording is appropriate. The best way to describe a neutral delivery style is that it cannot be identified as being from any particular country, being acceptable to all.

If music is used in the advertising, care should be taken that it is also acceptable to all groups. Preferred musical styles vary across nationality lines and even according to region within Mexico and with length of residence in the United States. Nevertheless, there are common musical themes that transcend nationality identification. The advertiser should also ensure that the commercial setting is not recognizably Mexican or Caribbean, but Hispanic. The same holds true in the portrayal of food.

Regionalizing a Hispanic campaign can be as simple as placing a different music track behind a common audio and/or video or as involved as producing different sets of commercials for each region in the United States according to Spanish nationality concentration, each with its own casting, setting, and language style.

Owing in part to production costs, the national approach is usually adopted in the development of a television campaign. In the case of a radio campaign, the regional approach is more common since production costs are much lower. The segmentation of audience in Spanish radio according to music preferences also lends itself to the regional approach, particularly in markets with a homogeneous Hispanic population.

Homogeneity in audience reached is crucial for the regional approach to be most successful. If the audience reached is heterogeneous, the advertiser would be appealing to a specific segment of the audience at the expense of reduced efficiency in persuading the other segments. A campaign that utilizes elements—language and music styles—that are strictly associated with one specific Spanish-origin group will not work well with other Spanish groups. The relative homogeneity of the Hispanic population in many local markets, however, works to the benefit of radio in this regard.

Some advertisers opt for using a combination of the national and regional philosophies in the development of the advertising campaign. This two-tier approach uses a national campaign on television and a regional campaign on radio in order to take advantage of each medium's qualities. Spanish radio focuses on the musical preferences of a local Hispanic audience that is generally homogeneous as to Spanish origin. Television's appeal, however, is less strictly focused on a specific Spanish nationality. Moreover, there is usually only one Spanish television station in the local market trying to appeal to the Hispanic audience as a whole as opposed to a number of Spanish radio stations, each with its own identity and audience.

When the same campaign is used in a number of markets, the national approach on television ensures that the advertising will effectively reach television's more diverse audience. The regional approach on radio takes advantage of radio's local focus and smoothly blends in with the regional speaking style of on-air personalities. When tag lines are given by a radio personality, compatability in speaking style is particularly effective. The regional approach on radio might be especially desirable when the advertiser wants to single out a specifically important Spanish-origin group in conjunction with a more generic Hispanic advertising campaign.

ADDITIONAL CONSIDERATIONS

The success of an advertising campaign can be significantly enhanced or diminished by considerations that are often only indirectly related to the commercial message that goes over the air. Elements as distant from the actual campaign as public relations efforts and available shelf space can play determinant roles in product acceptance and sales within the Hispanic market.

Public Relations

Sponsoring or participating in events such as festivals, parades, fairs, or "special days" that commemorate some aspect of the Hispanic community is an ideal way for a product or company to establish a presence in the local Hispanic community. These celebrations often center on a national Hispanic holiday such as Columbus Day or Mexican Independence Day. On other occasions, the celebrations arise from the proclamation of a special Hispanic Day by the local or regional government. At the federal level, Hispanic Heritage Week, falling in mid-September, has been proclaimed by the President of the United States yearly since 1974.

These types of activities have their greatest impact when the company or product becomes involved with the Hispanic community at the local level. An announcement in a national magazine or a tag in a broadcast commercial that recognizes Hispanic Heritage Week will be well-received. Sponsoring a concert or a parade at the local level, however, would much more effectively communicate a company's interest in Hispanics and its recognition of their worth as a people and as a market.

For an advertiser first coming into the Hispanic market or for an advertiser who is prevented from using the broadcast media, developing a rapport between the product and the Hispanic community at the local level can do as much for product image and sales as the most culturally attuned commercial on the air.

The public relations effort should ideally be coordinated and implemented by personnel from the product company and not from the advertising agency. Although the agency can be a very valuable ally and adviser, public relations is essentially outside of an advertising agency's primary expertise. Moreover, the personal participation of company staff gives the public relations effort a credibility it would otherwise not enjoy.

Distribution

Adequate distribution in the Hispanic market is by and large not a problem with most products. Outside of New York, Hispanics do most of their grocery shopping in supermarkets and establishments where the amount of shelf space allows for a wide selection of brands for each product. National as well as important regional brands are available in most stores where Hispanics do their shopping.

In the New York Hispanic market, however, product distribution can be a problem and should be regularly monitored. New York Hispanics do a great deal of their grocery shopping in *bodegas,* or small neighborhood stores. As a rule, *bodegas* are very limited in shelf space and will often carry only two or three brands of the same product, particularly if the product is a high-bulk item.

Sales in *bodegas* can represent 30 to 50 percent of the total New York Hispanic sales for certain products. If found to be necessary, the advertising agency and the Spanish station will generally work with the advertiser in developing and maintaining adequate distribution in the New York Hispanic market.

Coupons

Coupon use among Hispanics has traditionally been very low. The use of coupons is at times associated by Hispanics with the inability to purchase the product outright. For some Hispanics coupon use also implies that the buyer is not concerned with the quality of the product, but only with the price.

The low-prestige connotations of coupon use among Hispanics, however, appear to be changing. Coupons offered for recognizable, high-quality items are being increasingly redeemed. Among the Hispanic groups, Cubans, the highest-income Spanish-origin group in the United States, are particularly responsive to coupons, most likely because the low-prestige connotations of coupon use represent little threat to their self-esteem.

If coupons are offered in the Hispanic market, the instructions on how to make use of them should be simple, clear, direct, and in Spanish.

CONCLUSION

The U.S. Hispanic market is not homogeneous. It is a population composed of many interrelated and similar segments. The term "Hispanic" is an umbrella label encompassing all the various Spanish-speaking nationalities residing in the United States.

In terms of self-identification, the U.S. Hispanic may very well simultaneously perceive him- or herself not only as a member of a specific Spanish-speaking nationality such as Mexican, but also as a Hispanic and as an American, albeit in varying degrees of identification. Distinctions in U.S. Hispanic self-perception are evident in the variety of terms Hispanics use to describe themselves. Among the terms that do not refer to a specific nationality, "Hispanic," "Hispano," "Latino," and "Latin" are the most commonly used.

Using the reference to a specific Hispanic nationality as the common thread, a Cuban-origin Hispanic may, for example, identify with one or more of the following: "Cuban," "Cubano," "Cuban-American," and even an "American of Cuban descent." In the case of U.S. Hispanics from Mexico, there are the added terms "Chicano" and "Raza," both of which imply a certain political orientation in addition to Mexican origin. For Puerto Ricans, there is the recently coined "Newyorican," pointing to the inseparable blend of Puerto Rican and New York influences in an individual.

Were individual Hispanics asked to identify themselves, the majority would respond with a term that connotes a specific nationality or national origin: "Mexican" or "Mexican-American" or "Chicano," "Puerto Rican," "Cuban," "Dominican," "Venezuelan," "Colombian," etc. Only secondly would they refer to themselves by a nonnationality term such as "Hispanic" or "Latino." It is not surprising to discover that some general statements meant to apply to the Hispanic population as a whole or to a specific Hispanic population segment do not necessarily hold true for all U.S. Hispanic groups.

Among Hispanic respondents in the Yankelovich *Spanish USA* study conducted in 1981 for SIN–National Spanish Television Network, 61 percent said that some important differences exist among the various Hispanic-origin groups. On the other hand, 70 percent of the Hispanic respondents agreed or strongly agreed that because of the Spanish language, there was a strong common bond among the Hispanic-origin groups.

Differences do exist in Spanish speaking styles, music preferences, and favorite foods according to national origin. These differences notwithstanding, all Spanish-speaking nationalities in the United States share basic cultural values and traditions that are directly related to being Hispanic rather than to being from any single Spanish-speaking country. Just as the advertiser can develop effective advertising campaigns geared toward a single Spanish-origin group by making use of these differences, the advertiser can also develop effective advertising campaigns geared toward all Hispanics by making use of their commonalities.

From a marketing point of view, the term "U.S. Hispanic" is particularly useful in that it encompasses certain underlying cultural *and* demographic characteristics that are shared by all Hispanic nationalities living in the United States and that define the U.S. Hispanic market as distinct from the general population. More importantly, these shared cultural and demographic traits determine the attitudes and perceptions of U.S. Hispanics more than do the histories of their individual countries of origin.

Chapter 10

The Media Plan

In formulating the media plan for the U.S. Hispanic market, advertisers will find that they have few vehicles from which to choose in comparison with the general media. There are approximately 100 full-time Spanish-format radio stations and 12 television stations in the United States serving the Hispanic audience. Only the two largest Hispanic markets, New York and Los Angeles, have more than one Spanish television station. Spanish print, outdoor, and transit advertising are much less effective than broadcast advertising and should be used as supporting vehicles to a media plan centered on Spanish radio and television. Advertisements for products such as cigarettes and liquor that are prohibited from the broadcast media are the obvious exceptions to this rule.

The U.S. Hispanic market's strong broadcast orientation and the limited number of broadcast media outlets available simplify the development of the Hispanic media plan. Because of the Hispanic market's geographic concentration, the advertiser, whether at the national or at the local level, has to buy advertising time in few broadcast media in order to achieve effective coverage of the Hispanic audience. Monitoring of the advertising on the stations is also greatly facilitated.

Since the advertisers buy a relatively small number of stations, the schedules are concentrated and the advertisers can avail themselves of high-volume discounts. Additionally, the cost per thousand (CPM) in Spanish media is generally lower than in general-audience media. A major national television campaign can be mounted and sustained for 1 year at a cost of $1 million or less. A major national campaign on Spanish radio will run approximately $650,000 or less for 1 year.

The ability of both Spanish radio and Spanish television individually

141

to generate brand-share increases has been documented. When the advertiser is investing a limited amount of money, it may actually be preferable to regionalize the buy and concentrate it on one medium in order to maximize frequency levels. In this manner, the advertiser can also more easily determine the campaign's effect on business and the effectiveness of the medium used. When the advertiser makes a sufficient advertising investment, however, it is preferable to use a variety of media since each offers unique qualities.

There is little reason to establish an inflexible all-purpose rule as to the precise percentages of the advertising budget that should be assigned to each medium. Appropriate budget allocation weights vary according to the size of the overall budget and the effectiveness of the available media in reaching the target audience in the market area. The emphasis should nevertheless be placed on Spanish broadcasting whenever possible.

Ideally, the media plan will feature heavy radio and television schedules as well as print, outdoor, and transit advertising, each element reinforcing the others to communicate an integrated persuasion message. When the advertiser reaches the consumer through a variety of media, the total persuasion value of the campaign is enhanced as is the persuasion value of the individual advertising components.

TELEVISION[1]

As a medium, television offers the combination of sight and sound that places it, advertisement for advertisement, above the other media in its potential to persuade the consumer. Spanish television within the United States provides effective coverage in ten of the top fifteen U.S. Hispanic ADIs. Additionally, Spanish television stations in Mexico provide coverage of four important Hispanic border markets—San Diego, El Paso, Laredo, and El Centro–Yuma. The twelve U.S. Spanish television stations combined with the Mexican stations in the four border markets cover fourteen U.S markets with over 9.6 million Hispanics, or 65 percent of the Hispanic population within the United States.

SIN–National Spanish Television Network provides programming and serves as sales representative for ten of the fourteen U.S. Spanish stations. SIN is also the sales representative for four Mexican stations in the aforementioned border markets. Additionally, SIN's coverage is extended by a network of cable system and translator affiliates (over 100 by 1982) carrying the SIN signal. SIN expects to double that figure by 1983. Most of SIN's affiliates are satellite-interconnected and transmit Spanish programming 24 hours a day, 7 days a week.

[1] See Listings—Spanish-Format Television Stations, in Chapter 4, for individual listings of television stations.

SIN's addition of the cable system and translator affiliates has certainly added tens, if not hundreds, of thousands of regular viewers to the network. It is open to question, however, whether these affiliates provide effective coverage in each of their market areas. The cable affiliates cover only those Hispanic households in their areas that subscribe to the system. The translator affiliates are currently prohibited by the FCC from operating at a power above 1 kilowatt. The FCC may waive the limitation in some cases or allow all translators to operate at higher power in the future. In general, at their current power level, however, translators transmit too weak a signal to effectively reach the total coverage area encompassed by the ADIs in which they operate. In the cases of both cable and translator affiliates, actual audience estimates per program are very difficult to ascertain.

Advertisers can purchase advertising on SIN stations on a network or a spot basis. When buying advertising on a network basis, the advertiser receives a substantial reduction from the cumulative spot price. Advertisers interested in a number of Spanish television markets can also obtain a break in price by buying a combination of stations without having to buy the entire network.

Sales Offices

New York: 250 Park Ave., New York, NY 10177, (212) 953-7500

Chicago: 230 N. Michigan Ave., Chicago, IL 60601, (312) 782-1129

Los Angeles: 5358 Melrose Ave., Los Angeles, CA 90038, (213) 463-2152

Miami: 2525 S.W. Third Ave., Miami, FL 33129, (305) 856-2793

Dallas: 3626 N. Hall St., Dallas, TX 75219, (214) 528-8161

San Francisco: 2200 Palou Ave., San Francisco, CA 94124, (415) 641-1400

The two independent Spanish television stations currently in operation in the United States are also available to the advertiser as a package. WNJU-TV in New York and KBSC-TV in Los Angeles are both owned by Oak Broadcasting System. The two stations combined reach a potential Hispanic audience of more than 4.5 million, or 31 percent of the total U.S. Hispanic population. KBSC-TV in Los Angeles is not full-time Spanish since it changes to over-the-air subscription television in the evenings. The possibility exists that KBSC-TV will go Spanish full-time in the future.

Sales Offices

New York: WNJU-TV, 425 Park Ave., New York, NY 10022, (212) 935-3480

Los Angeles: KBSC-TV, 1139 Grand Central Ave., Glendale, CA 91201, (213) 507-6522

Chicago: 20 N. Wacker Dr., Suite 540, Chicago, IL 60606, (312) 263-3340

Atlanta: 3384 Peachtree Rd., N.E., Suite 417, Atlanta, GA 30326, (404) 237-1577

Beginning in April 1981 and offering Spanish-language programming via cable systems in the Houston area, Spanish Universal Network (SUN) has expanded its coverage to three additional market areas in less than 1 year. Broadcasting out of Matamoros, Mexico, on XRIO-TV, channel 23, SUN covers the Texas Rio Grande valley, reaching McAllen, Harlingen, and Brownsville on the U.S. side of the Mexican border. El Paso, Texas, and Las Cruces, New Mexico, are covered by XHRJ-TV, channel 44, out of Ciudad Juarez. SUN expects to be transmitting its programming via satellite by mid-1982.

Sales Office

Spanish Universal Network, Inc., 2400 Augusta, Suite 350, Houston, TX 77057, (713) 974-1497

A fairly recent phenomenon in Spanish television programming has been the emergence of the Spanish language syndicated program. Usually carried by English stations, these syndicated shows are broadcast in a number of cities at varying time periods and offer still another television alternative to the advertiser.

The best known of these programs is *The Val De La O Television Show,* currently aired in twenty-eight markets with additional coverage provided by cable and translator affiliates.

Sales Office

Val De La O Productions, Inc., 2017 San Mateo, N.E., Albuquerque, NM 87110, (505) 265-6626

RADIO[2]

Spanish radio covers virtually 100 percent of the Hispanic population in the United States with at least one full-time Spanish radio station operating in over fifty U.S. Hispanic markets. In markets with large Hispanic populations, the advertiser usually has a choice of two, three,

---

[2] See Listings—Spanish-Format Radio Stations, in Chapter 3, for individual listings of radio stations.

or more Spanish radio stations. Miami, for example, has seven stations vying for the Hispanic listening audience.

A primary strength of Spanish radio is its ability and willingness to tie merchandising efforts to the advertising schedule. Spanish radio personnel will work closely with the advertiser in providing support for promotions or contests. Many will also work with the advertiser in achieving proper distribution in markets such as New York, where distribution might be a problem owing to the small shelf space capacity of some stores with a primarily Hispanic clientele. Spanish radio also enjoys a strong person-to-person relationship with the listener that can be used to great advantage by featuring local station personalities in the commercials. The use of local on-air personalities tends to give the commercial message a quality of personal advice to the regular listener. Since each personality has an individual style, however, the advertising might lose some of its sense of uniformity or continuity.

The largest national sales representative of Spanish-format stations in the United States is Caballero Spanish Media. Caballero represents over fifty Spanish radio stations covering forty markets across the nation. These forty markets encompass 95 percent of the U.S. Hispanic population. Caballero also provides support in the coordination of advertiser merchandising efforts with the local radio station.

Advertisers can buy time on the Caballero Radio Network on a spot or network basis, with the network rate being lower than the cumulative spot cost. To avail themselves of the network rate, advertisers must buy a minimum of five markets with a schedule of at least twelve announcements per week in each market. Minimum requirements do not apply when buying on a spot basis. Getting the network rate without having to buy more than five markets gives the advertiser a great deal of flexibility in the design of the media plan.

Sales Offices

New York: 30 E. 42d St., New York, NY 10017, (212) 972-1019

Chicago: 20 N. Wacker Dr., Chicago, IL 60606, (312) 263-3340

Los Angeles: 5724 Hollywood Blvd., Los Angeles, CA 90028, (213) 465-8337

Atlanta: 1819 Peachtree Rd., N.E., Atlanta, GA 30309, (404) 355-6432

Dallas: 5480 Denton Drive Cutoff, Dallas, TX 75235, (214) 630-6397

Lotus Reps, a division of Lotus Communications Corporation, represents over forty Spanish radio stations in thirty-four different markets through the Lotus Spanish Network. Lotus-represented stations reach up to 11 million Hispanics, encompassing approximately 73 percent of the national Hispanic population.

Sales Offices

New York: 50 E. 42d St., New York, NY 10017, (212) 697-7601

Chicago: 203 N. Wabash Ave., Chicago, IL 60601, (312) 346-8442

Los Angeles: 6777 Hollywood Blvd., Hollywood, CA 90028, (213) 466-8119

San Francisco: 105 Montgomery St., San Francisco, CA 94104, (415) 398-2164

Dallas: 3225 Lemon Ave., Dallas, TX 75205, (214) 528-7151

While Caballero and Lotus are the largest, there are additional national and regional rep firms that represent groups of Spanish radio stations throughout the United States. One of the better-known firms, the Southwest Spanish Broadcast Group, represents a total of fourteen stations in Texas, California, Arizona, Colorado, and New Mexico.

Sales Office

Albuquerque: P.O. Box 4486, Albuquerque, NM 87196, (505) 243-1744

PRINT[3]

As a supporting medium, Spanish print can communicate a vast amount of information and a degree of detail that is not feasible through broadcasting. When the advertiser desires a large amount of copy to tell the product's story—through a new recipe for a food product, for example—print provides the space at a low cost. Conversely, a strong visual advertisement in Spanish print provides a viable visual impact to complement a radio campaign.

Spanish print is an effective tool for promoting contests and sweepstakes and for distributing coupons. Spanish magazines segment the Hispanic audience, making it possible for advertisers to reach the exact type of consumer they want to reach, without having to pay for extraneous circulation. Spanish newspapers are effective advertising vehicles for supermarkets, restaurants, theaters, and other local retailers, particularly when they feature special sales announcements.

[3] Publisher information for individual Spanish magazines and newspapers is provided in Chapter 2 under Listings—Spanish Magazines and Listings—Spanish Newspapers, respectively.

De Armas Publications represents over a dozen Spanish language magazines with distribution in the major Hispanic population centers in the United States and throughout Latin America. While the editorial content of most De Armas publications is oriented toward the Hispanic woman, a few publications go after the Hispanic male market. Advertisers can buy space in individual magazines or in a combination of De Armas–represented publications. Regional editions of De Armas magazines are available in which space can be bought at a discount. Discounts are also given when the advertiser buys space in a number of publications.

Sales Offices

New York: De Armas Publications, 605 Third Ave., Suite 1620, New York, NY 10158, (212) 687-8760

Miami: Editorial America, S.A., Vanidades Continental Building, 6355 N.W. 36th St., Virginia Gardens, FL 33166, (305) 871-6400

OUTDOOR AND TRANSIT ADVERTISING

Outdoor and transit advertising can be very effective in complementing a broadcast-intensive campaign. To complement a radio campaign, outdoor and transit ads can provide the advertiser with a strong visual presence at a low cost. The concentration of the Hispanic population in specific neighborhoods enables Spanish outdoor advertising in particular to be used effectively to reach the intended Hispanic target. Transit advertising can also be effective when strategically placed in routes with high Hispanic traffic; however, the advertiser will wind up paying for non-Hispanic traffic as well.

Becoming familiar with where the local Hispanic community lives and with its use of public transportation is a basic prerequisite for the advertiser planning to use outdoor or transit displays. Maximizing Hispanic traffic while minimizing non-Hispanic traffic is the key to the cost-effective utilization of Spanish outdoor and transit advertising.

RATINGS

The accurate measurement of the Hispanic broadcast audience is an open question for Spanish broadcasters and advertisers alike. Some Spanish broadcasters charge that A. C. Nielsen and Arbitron are significantly underrepresenting their audiences; others assert just as strongly that conventional general-market surveys do a credible job of reflecting the Hispanic audience. Some advertisers buy advertising time strictly on the basis of Nielsen and Arbitron ratings; others make adjustments to the advertising time they buy by consulting Hispanic-audience measurements from other sources. Hispanic-audience measurements conducted by Strategy Research Corporation have gained some degree of acceptance among advertisers, for instance.

Arbitron and Nielsen enjoy a very high degree of built-in ratings credibility in the broadcasting and advertising industries. Their reputations are based on long years of dependable service in providing general-audience ratings. When advertisers want to know the audience of a program, they ask for "the book," meaning the Arbitron or Nielsen book. Seldom is another source consulted. When other sources are consulted, the credibility of their Hispanic-audience measurements often depends on how closely these measurements reflect the ratings reported by Nielsen and Arbitron. In a sense, Nielsen and Arbitron have become their own standards of ratings accuracy.

The perceived credibility and accuracy of Nielsen and Arbitron ratings are well-deserved in the measurement of the general audience. It is not so well deserved in their measurement of the Hispanic audience owing to factors both within and outside of their direct control.

The Hispanic population figures used by Nielsen and Arbitron in their audience surveys are believed by many to be too conservative. Since special Hispanic methodologies are instituted according to Hispanic concentration in the survey area, some Spanish broadcasters claim that these special methodologies are not used as extensively as they should be, contributing to a Hispanic-audience undercount. Because of the difficulties in arriving at widely accepted and accurate Hispanic population figures, made especially difficult because of the Hispanic undocumented alien segment, this is a problem that is not shared by Nielsen and Arbitron alone.

Criticism of their Hispanic-audience measurements, however, extends to the special methodologies utilized after it has been determined that Hispanic concentration in the survey area is high enough to warrant their use.

Special Hispanic methodologies have been instituted largely as a result of the low level of ratings-diary return from Hispanic homes. The rate of diary return in the general population is approximately 55 percent of the diaries placed in the home. The rate of diary return from Hispanic homes is between 15 and 25 percent of the diaries placed. This low level of return leads some critics to believe that the Hispanic diaries being returned are not representative of the Hispanic population's viewing and listening habits.

The first contact made by Nielsen and Arbitron when attempting to place a diary in the Hispanic home is initiated in English. Should the respondent answer in Spanish, the interviewer switches to Spanish, if he or she is bilingual. If the placement interviewer is not bilingual, the telephone headset is handed to an operator who does speak Spanish or else the respondent is called back later by a Spanish language operator.

Given the initial use of English by the placement interviewer, the Hispanic respondent might feel some pressure to respond in English, even if he or she feels more comfortable speaking Spanish. This English language atmosphere may influence the choice of language used by self-identified Hispanic homes to fill out the diaries and may indirectly bias the choice of programming recorded.

For example, in February 1977, Nielsen conducted special studies of self-identified Spanish-speaking homes in Laredo and El Paso, Texas. In Laredo, 87 percent of these homes returned a diary in English. In El Paso, 75 percent returned an English diary. This high incidence of English language–diary return is somewhat incongruous with the identification of the sample as representative of Spanish-speaking homes in those areas.

In an effort to upgrade measurement of the Hispanic audience, Arbitron instituted the personal placement and retrieval (PPR) technique in the metropolitan areas of New York, Miami, Los Angeles, San Antonio, Albuquerque, Corpus Christi, El Paso, and McAllen-Brownsville. The PPR technique consists of personally placing the diary, personally monitoring its maintenance at midweek, and personally retrieving the diary at the end of the survey period.

The PPR technique also addresses the problem of surveying nontelephone Hispanic homes. The Arbitron PPR technique begins with a telephone base, then includes the home next door at the time of placement, potentially adding nontelephone homes. It is unknown, however, whether the number of nontelephone homes surveyed has any relevance to the incidence of nontelephone homes in the Hispanic population being measured.

The PPR technique has significantly raised the diary response rate among Hispanic homes, but its use is limited to metropolitan areas, not complete ADIs, and only within census tracts with Hispanic-population penetration of 35 percent or more.

Arbitron has been experimenting with an alternative procedure, differential survey treatments (DST). Under DST, Arbitron places the diaries only by phone, offers a premium for diaries returned by mail, and increases its follow-up calls. DST has the advantage of being utilized throughout the entire metropolitan area, but results in a slightly lower diary return rate among Hispanics than in the rest of the market and excludes nontelephone homes from the survey sample. There is a high probability that Arbitron will implement the DST procedure as a regular part of its audience measurement of Hispanics in some markets.

The methodologies used by Nielsen and Arbitron to measure the Hispanic audience have their limitations; they do not reflect the Hispanic audience with the same degree of accuracy that they reflect the general audience. They do, however, provide a valid indication of audience. The Spanish station with the largest Hispanic audience in the market will in all likelihood be reported in the number 1 position among Spanish stations by Arbitron and Nielsen. The Spanish station's actual audience is probably larger than what Arbitron and Nielsen report, but its place among the Spanish stations in the market should hold true. If there is a tendency to underrepresent the Hispanic audience—and there probably is—the degree of underrepresentation should be uniform among all the Spanish stations in the survey area.

This likely underrepresentation means that the advertiser is probably reaching a larger Hispanic audience than that reflected by Arbitron and Nielsen for Spanish stations. Moreover, it means that the costs per thousand on Spanish stations are probably lower than the Arbitron and Nielsen ratings would indicate.

Converting General-Audience Ratings to Hispanic Ratings

Arbitron and Nielsen ratings represent the percentage of the total audience in the survey area viewing or listening to a station at any given time period. The advertiser can use Nielsen and Arbitron ratings, however, to arrive at a Spanish station's percentage of audience within the Hispanic market only, i.e., the station's Hispanic rating.

This can be done through a simple process of conversion. All that is necessary is to relate the Spanish station's actual audience in numbers to the Hispanic population universe in the survey area, as the following model explains.

Let a theoretical market have a total population of 2.8 million people, 700,000 of whom are Hispanics.

Total market   Hispanic market
universe = 2,800,000   universe = 700,000

The market has two Spanish stations—stations A and B—in addition to several general-market stations. The Arbitron or Nielsen ratings, i.e., total market ratings, are 6.8 for station A and 4.5 for station B.

Arbitron or Nielsen rating for   Arbitron or Nielsen rating for
Spanish station A = 6.8   Spanish station B = 4.5

Considering the total market universe, we find that station A has an actual audience of 190,400 and that station B has an audience of 126,000 during a particular time period.

2,800,000	(total market)	2,800,000	(total market)
×6.8%	(rating)	×4.5%	(rating)
190,400	(actual audience for station A)	126,000	(actual audience for station B)

The audiences for stations A and B are now each divided by the number of people in the Hispanic market universe in order to arrive at the Hispanic market ratings of 27.2 for station A and 18.0 for station B. (The advertiser can safely assume that the audiences for Spanish stations A and B are Hispanic.)

$$\frac{190,400 \text{ (actual audience)}}{700,000 \text{ (Hispanic market)}} = 27.2 \text{ (Hispanic rating for Spanish station A)}$$

$$\frac{126,000 \text{ (actual audience)}}{700,000 \text{ (Hispanic market)}} = 18.0 \text{ (Hispanic rating for Spanish station B)}$$

The Hispanic ratings represent the percentages of the Hispanic audience for stations A and B, respectively, for the time period during which the stations were rated.

That is the longhand logic behind the conversion of total market ratings to Hispanic market ratings. The advertiser, however, does not have to go through this long process in order to convert the ratings. All that is really necessary is to determine the relation between the total market universe and the Hispanic market universe and to apply this factor to the total market ratings.

In our theoretical model, the total market universe is four times larger than the Hispanic market universe.

$$\frac{2,800,000 \text{ (total market universe)}}{700,000 \text{ (Hispanic market universe)}} = 4 \text{ (Hispanic factor)}$$

Once the Hispanic factor has been determined, it is a simple matter to multiply the Arbitron or Nielsen ratings—the total market ratings—by the Hispanic factor (in this case, 4) to arrive at the Hispanic market rating.

6.8	(rating)	4.5	(rating)
×4	(Hispanic factor)	×4	(Hispanic factor)
27.2	(Hispanic market rating for Spanish station A)	18.0	(Hispanic market rating for Spanish station B)

Naturally, the relation between the total market universe and Hispanic market universe will vary according to the demographic unit that the advertiser wishes to reach. The relation between total market persons and Hispanic market persons will in almost every case be different from that between total market households and Hispanic market households, for instance. The correct Hispanic factor has to be individually determined for each demographic segment, for instance, relating total market women 18 to 34 years old to Hispanic market women of the same age group.

The principle used to determine Hispanic market ratings on the basis of total market audience data cannot be used to calculate Hispanic market audience shares. Since there is no way of distinguishing the number of Hispanics using English language media from the total market data, it is impossible to ascertain the total number of Hispanics listening to the radio or watching television at any given time period. Consequently, the relation between Spanish-station audience and the total Hispanic audience using the media cannot be established.

REACH AND FREQUENCY

A Spanish station will generally have a higher reach in the Hispanic market than a comparable general-audience station will have in the total market audience. This is a direct function of the small number of Spanish stations usually vying for the Hispanic audience in comparison with the number of general-audience stations competing for the total market audience. The segmentation of the Hispanic audience by stations is usually kept to a minimum.

The high target-audience reach of Spanish stations, however, is influenced by differences in Hispanic and non-Hispanic media habits. These differences result in a lower target-audience reach for Spanish stations than one would expect for general-audience stations given a comparable situation in the general market. Hispanic listeners and viewers are very loyal to their favorite stations, resulting in relatively low Hispanic-audience crossover between Spanish stations in comparison with non-Hispanic crossover between general-audience stations. This is particularly true for Spanish radio because Hispanic *listener* loyalty is to the station itself, whereas Hispanic *viewer* loyalty is more toward specific programs.

Given identical numbers of Spanish and general-audience stations competing for an audience that is 50 percent Hispanic and 50 percent non-Hispanic, the Spanish station would generally have a lower reach within the Hispanic 50 percent of the total audience than a comparable general-audience station would have within the non-Hispanic 50 percent of the total audience.

For example, market A may have five Spanish stations and five general-audience stations and a Hispanic and non-Hispanic audience of equal proportions. The Hispanic-audience reach of a Spanish station may be lower than the respective non-Hispanic reach of a general-audience station with non-Hispanic ratings that are identical to the Hispanic ratings of the Spanish station.

This is seldom the case, however, as general-audience stations generally far outnumber the Spanish stations in the market, creating much greater audience segmentation in the general audience than exists in the Hispanic audience. As a rule, Spanish stations enjoy a high reach within the Hispanic market because of their small numbers.

The differences in Hispanic and non-Hispanic media habits related to audience crossover mean that the unduplicated audiences reported by Nielsen and Arbitron for Spanish stations are based on principles that may not pertain to the Hispanic audience. If based on general-audience behavior, the unduplicated audience for the Spanish stations may be smaller than that reflected by Arbitron and Nielsen. On the other hand, Arbitron's and Nielsen's likely underrepresentation of the Spanish station's ratings—partly due to methodological limitations—tends to compensate for this possible overstatement of the Spanish station's unduplicated audience.

The advertiser can arrive at a reasonable indication of the Spanish station's reach in the Hispanic market by using Arbitron's and Nielsen's unduplicated-audience figures. To determine Hispanic reach, the Spanish station's unduplicated audience is divided by the Hispanic market universe.

Using the same theoretical market as before—a total market universe of 2,800,000 and a Hispanic market universe of 700,000—an unduplicated audience of 325,000 for Spanish station A would represent a reach of 11.6 percent in the total market universe. The Spanish station's reach in the Hispanic market universe would be 46.4 percent.

$$\frac{325,000 \text{ (unduplicated audience)}}{2,800,000 \text{ (total market universe)}} = 11.6\% \text{ (total market reach)}$$

$$\frac{325,000 \text{ (unduplicated audience)}}{700,000 \text{ (Hispanic market universe)}} = 46.4\% \text{ (Hispanic market reach)}$$

As is the case with the conversion of total market ratings to Hispanic market ratings, each unduplicated-audience figure is to be related to its corresponding demographic segment in the Hispanic market.

An advertising schedule on a Spanish station will provide frequency levels within the Hispanic audience that are probably higher than the ratings would indicate.

Owing to the Hispanic audience's strong station loyalty, the unduplicated audience of the Spanish station diminishes at a faster rate than it does for general-audience stations. For example, 1000 gross ratings points (GRPs) on a general-audience station would produce significantly lower frequency levels in the total market universe than 1000 Hispanic GRPs on a Spanish station would produce in the Hispanic market universe.

This can be used to the advertiser's advantage because a Hispanic campaign requires high frequency levels in order to be most effective. First, the advertiser is usually addressing a market that has received little attention from the product brand in the past, so it is very important to create a strong and constant presence. Secondly, Hispanics are very brand-loyal in their purchasing habits. Advertisers must therefore constantly communicate and reinforce the message to try their brand in order to change Hispanic brand-buying habits and increase their share of the market.

CONCLUSION

Spanish media's comparatively lower costs mean that the advertiser can reach more Hispanic consumers than general market consumers for the same advertising expenditure. The small number of media that cater to the Hispanic audience means that the advertiser has to buy advertising in relatively few media outlets in order to reach a significant segment of the market.

Much higher frequency levels can be achieved in the Hispanic market than in the general market for disproportionately lower advertising costs. In combination with the lower level of advertising competition in the Hispanic market as compared with the general market, this means that the advertiser can gain an impressive domination in share of voice in the product category for a relatively limited investment.

Chapter 11

Scott Paper Company— Case History

The Scott Paper Company's experience in the U.S. Hispanic market began before 1970 when they used Spanish advertising behind campaigns for Viva, Baby Scott, and Scot Tissue. This specialized effort—much of it based on "best guesses" about effectiveness and efficiency—had been almost an afterthought, had never been analyzed, and was at least 5 years old when, in 1975, Scott began the research stage with the Hispanic market.

Scott's objective was to identify special opportunities open to their particular product line and then implement marketing activity that would address those opportunities.

Initially, Scott asked itself three basic questions and developed some answers:

Question 1: How certain are we that we are marketing in an intelligent way to the Hispanic population in the United States?

Answer: Not at all certain, because we have essentially no information about our products or our products' acceptance in that market.

Question 2: Do we need a specialized resource to help us to explore the Hispanic market and to merchandise products in it?

Answer: Probably, because several factors make this a specialized marketing opportunity, not the least of which are language and cultural differences.

(After exploration with several groups offering specialized services and after talking with some other packaged goods manufacturers who had worked in the market, Scott chose a Hispanic advertising agency to handle this specialized effort.)

Question 3: Are there differences in the purchase and use of paper products between the general and the Hispanic markets?

Answer: Probably, so let us conduct some research into the market.

The decision to do research raised some immediate issues for Scott, for example, the specific wording to be used in the research—what do Hispanics call toilet tissue and paper towels? There seemed to be more than one term, and Scott was not certain which one would be best to use. Obviously, it was important to use the correct term in order to obtain valid responses to the research.

Scott answered the question with some fast pilot research and was then ready to obtain answers to key market questions. Scott approached the respondents by asking open-ended questions, followed by aided questions about particular characteristics:

- What paper products do Hispanics use?

- What do Hispanics like about the products that they now use? What don't they like about these products or about the products that they have tried previously? For instance, when Hispanics describe the product attributes that are important in making a choice between similar products, what are these attributes? How do they rank? How important are strength, softness, and absorbency—attributes that loom as highly important in all the general market research done by Scott?

- What about packaging? Some of the products come in one, two, four, or more rolls, big or small rolls, and large or small sizes. Which of these are most favored by the Hispanic consumer and why?

- What about color choices for the product? Scott has white and pastels. Do Hispanics like strong colors or light colors?

- Some products allow mixing and matching with accessories. How important is that?

- There are numerous design choices, particularly for boxes of facial tissues. Are Scott's designs in keeping with the aesthetic senses of the Hispanic consumer?

- How about design choices in the products themselves? Scott has towels that have decorated borders and towels that are decorated all over, as well as bathroom tissue with decoration on it. What do Hispanics think about these?

- How about scent? Is scent good or is it bad? In which types of paper products is it desired and not desired?

- What about economy? How important is it? What are the product features that appear to deliver economy? How does the consumer recognize that economy has been delivered or is promised?

- What about convenience—convenience in the purchase quantity, convenience in storage, convenience in not running out just when the consumer needs the product?

- How much of a given product is used per month? How much of a given product is bought per purchase?

- When the product is in the home, how is it used? For what different things? Does usage vary with the person in the family doing the task? This variation would be especially likely with paper towels.

- Does the name "Scott" mean anything to the Hispanic community? Colgate has strong favorable impressions for many products, but does Scott mean anything, and, if so, how should it be identified or associated with the products?

- Are there differences in attitudes toward products that have the name "Scott" in the product name—ScotTowels, for example—and those that simply have a manufacturer line on the package?

- Do Hispanics understand the use of coupons and other promotion incentives? Do they appreciate them as opportunities to save money? What kinds of promotions interest Hispanics most? What kind of involvement can be expected when a given promotional incentive is made available?

- What do Hispanics think about brands that are not advertised versus brands that are advertised? Is being an advertised brand a particular asset in the Hispanic community?

The possible questions were seemingly endless. Just compiling the questionnaire reinforced Scott's conviction that it had quite a bit to learn about the perception and acceptance of its products in the Hispanic market—and Scott *did* learn a lot.

To complement the information it had compiled on its products, Scott gathered information on the Hispanic people and asked the market a different series of questions:

- What are the age distributions of Hispanics? Their family sizes and composition? Their jobs, income, and education? What language do they speak? If they speak both English and Spanish, where do they speak each?

- What are their media habits? What television stations do they watch? When and where do they watch television? What radio stations do they listen to? When and where do they listen to the radio? What print media do they read? With which do they feel most confident? Which, in their opinion, provides the best information?

- How does all this relate to instructions on the product package or to information provided at the point of purchase for a product?

Once Scott had obtained the answers to these questions, it had a solid and valid body of information—about product characteristics, product habits, and the Hispanic market itself—upon which to base sound marketing decisions.

Scott then approached the second stage, the action stage—deciding what to do with the information obtained from the research.

Scott concluded that it needed to prepare a separate product position statement for each of the brands for which it would consider special marketing efforts to the Hispanic community. The product position statement would identify the relevant competition, the relevant product opportunities as perceived by Scott, and the objective of the marketing activity.

Next, Scott prepared a separate copy-strategy statement especially for the Hispanic consumer. This statement provided creative direction for the advertising by identifying the principal reason or reasons why Scott would expect a Hispanic consumer to purchase its product over a competitive product.

Scott observed that while specific recommendations varied according to product, some common elements emerged. Scott noted that the advertising should be very strong in awareness building and that it should address one primary selling idea. At least in radio, however, Scott decided that there was an opportunity to address one or more secondary product or performance features because the nature of the sale and the length of the message permitted it. Finally, Scott realized that there was an obligation to be authentic in the casting, the setting, and the language used in the advertising.

Broadcast advertising was created for three products—a new product, an established product, and a long-established product. Scott used Hispanic talent, producers, and directors, following normal production requirements.

Based on its knowledge of Spanish media habits, Scott elected to concentrate on radio and television advertising. For two of the products, Scott did use limited newspaper and billboard advertising as special support activities.

Development of the best possible media plan was hampered by what Scott found to be a lack of accurate and reliable data on Hispanic audience behavior, market ratings, market reach, and frequency levels. This lack of data also made it harder to sell the plan to the brand manager. Brand managers are constantly faced with a number of opportunities calling for an investment of advertising and communications dollars. Brand managers therefore require the best information possible in order to choose correctly from the available opportunities. The relatively lower amount of information available on the Hispanic market works against it.

Scott assessed the prepared advertising on the basis of judgment alone because it did not know how to assess it otherwise. Scott felt that none of the attention, recall, or impact methods which it regularly used to assess its general-audience advertising were readily adaptable to the Hispanic market.

Scott, however, felt that a measure of the advertising's effectiveness was necessary and explored how it could do this. Scott believed that there were no reliable sales data that could be generated specifically for the Hispanic market. The Scott field sales force did not have access to special Hispanic market shipment, sales, or warehouse withdrawal data. They could not identify any other mechanism to provide such data, and there appeared to be no rating service which could provide data on a purchase basis.

As a result, Scott decided to do some tracking research at least. It was making an investment that it wanted to pay off, and it wanted to have as much measurement assistance as possible in order to identify the nature of the payoff. Scott finally settled on using three key measures which in its judgment would significantly reflect actual sales volume.

Scott chose to measure (1) *brand awareness,* measuring both the number of respondents for whom a particular Scott product came to mind first and the total number at least aware of that product, though not necessarily mentioning it first; (2) *advertising awareness,* again, measuring both first-to-mind and total awareness of Scott advertisements for particular products; and (3) *brand bought most often,* reflecting the percentage of respondents buying a particular Scott product more often than other brands.

Scott's objective was to increase, significantly, the brands' positions in all of these three measured areas. Prior to the start of the advertising campaign, Scott took a reading in selected market areas. It then ran what was a meaningful, if not dramatic, advertising schedule, and it conducted telephone research after a reasonable amount of effort had been placed in the advertising activity.

Following are the actual results obtained by Scott on each of the three key measures for the three different products.

Product A—New Product

	Before advertising (%)	After 12 months of advertising (%)
Brand awareness:		
First mention	0	12
Total	3	24
Advertising awareness:		
Unaided	0	20
Total	0	56
Brand bought most often	0	12

Product B—Established Product

	Before advertising (%)	After 10 months of advertising (%)
Brand awareness:		
First mention	14	24
Total	47	65
Advertising awareness:		
Unaided	0	48
Total	0	65
Brand bought most often	15	40

Product C—Long-Established Product

	Before advertising (%)	After 24 months of advertising (%)
Brand Awareness:		
First mention	35	47
Advertising awareness:		
Unaided	0	29
Brand bought most often	37	51

From these results, Scott decided that something had obviously happened in the marketplace and that it had achieved its objective—a significant increase in each of the measured areas. Scott did not know what degree of increase it should have expected but concluded that what it got was significant.

On one of the brands, Scott did not continue its advertising schedule as originally planned owing to budget problems and saw the numbers decline significantly. In another instance, the arrival of a new competitor backed by general-audience and Hispanic advertising led to a significant decline in the Scott-brand numbers.

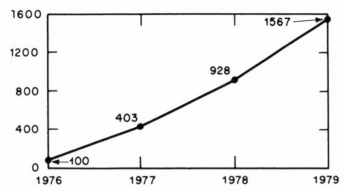

Figure 11-1   Scott Paper Company spending in the Hispanic market (indexed base = 100).

Recognizing the need for continued, meaningful advertising support, Scott has followed its initial experiences with increased budgets for Hispanic marketing since 1975 (see Figure 11-1).

The Scott Paper Company's case history in the Hispanic market is typical of many companies' experience in the market. After years of making what was essentially a token effort in the market and not knowing whether it was getting any results, Scott made the decision to approach the Hispanic market as a business opportunity. Finding much less information on the Hispanic market than it was accustomed to having on the general market, Scott initially invested in basic product and Hispanic market research upon which to base its marketing and advertising strategies.

Having decided to advertise in the market, Scott sought an advertising agency with experience in the field to work on the development and implementation of the creative strategy and the media plan—a creative strategy that resulted in finished advertising which Scott initially assessed on the basis of its judgment alone and that resulted in a media plan based on less than incontestable audience data. Therefore, it became particularly important for Scott to arrive at some valid measure of the advertising campaign's effect on the marketplace. Scott settled on brand and advertising awareness and brand bought most often as measuring standards.

In spite of the difficulties in ascertaining Hispanic advertising's direct impact on Scott business, the measurements taken provided sufficient evidence in Scott's eyes to justify the initial investment. Indeed, Scott's Hispanic advertising budget has dramatically increased since 1975 even though Scott remains somewhat uncomfortable with the idea that the effect of Hispanic advertising on sales cannot be substantiated to the same degree that the effect of general advertising can.

Chapter 12

Trends and Projections

Today, the U.S. Hispanic population is younger, has larger families, and is more geographically concentrated than the non-Hispanic population. The U.S. Hispanic population also has lower income, lesser-quality employment, and lower educational attainment than does the general population.

During the 1980s, the U.S. Hispanic population will continue to be younger and to have larger families than the non-Hispanic population, although the size of both Hispanic and non-Hispanic families is expected to decrease. The geographic concentration of the Hispanic population is expected to persist and possibly increase as the existing Hispanic concentrations in primarily urban centers act as magnets, attracting other Hispanics through the pull of familiar language and culture.

Differences in income, education, and employment will also remain, although the gap between the Hispanic and non-Hispanic populations will probably narrow. The relationship between Hispanic and non-Hispanic median income has been relatively stable from 1971 to 1980, with Hispanic median family income at approximately 70 percent that of the general population. However, increased educational and employment opportunities for Hispanics in the 1980s will likely narrow the existing gap.

During the 1980s, the 31 percent of the total Hispanic population that is now between the ages of 18 and 34 will experience the peak earning years in their lives, and many of the 13.1 percent of the total Hispanic population who are now teenagers will be entering the work force and developing their careers. Many of these Hispanics will have employment opportunities open to them which were not available to Hispanics in the past.

The Hispanics now working and those entering the work force during the 1980s are better prepared educationally and professionally to undertake a wider variety of jobs and careers than Hispanics have been in the past. The greater emphasis on education among young Hispanics is already evident in the dramatic increase in educational attainment seen for Hispanics 20 to 24 years old as compared with Hispanics 25 years old. Of Hispanics 25 and older, 43 percent have at least finished high school as compared with 64 percent of Hispanics 20 to 24 years old. Many of the 20- to 24-year-old Hispanics are now in the process of completing higher education. This trend indicates a future increase in the quantity and quality of Hispanic employment, which will in turn contribute toward an increase in Hispanic median income.

The degree to which the income, education, and employment gaps will narrow largely depends on the status of the U.S. economy during the 1980s. Since many Hispanics will first be entering the work force during the 1980s and many other Hispanics will not enjoy the seniority of non-Hispanics, it will be the Hispanic worker who will be one of the most directly and negatively affected segments of the work force during times of economic decline or nongrowth. Should an economic downturn occur, the repercussions will be felt quickly in the income and educational levels of the Hispanic population.

The one demographic trend above all others that will mold the future of the U.S. Hispanic community through the 1980s and beyond is its numerical growth. In the 10 years between 1970 and 1980, the Hispanic population in the United States increased 65 percent, from 9 million in 1970 to approximately 15 million in 1980. Were the same rate of growth to continue until the end of the century, the U.S. Hispanic population would be 20 million by 1986, approach 25 million by 1990, and exceed the 40 million mark by the year 2000.

Taking into account the current Hispanic undocumented population of 7.4 million in these projections, the total U.S. Hispanic population would be 22.4 million in 1980, exceed 31 million by 1986, approach 37 million by 1990, and exceed 60 million by the turn of the century.

Given the higher birthrate of the U.S. Hispanic population as compared with the general population, the large size of the Hispanic family, the comparative youth of the U.S. Hispanic population, and the fact that legal and illegal immigration to the United States from Spanish-speaking countries shows no sign of slackening, a U.S. Hispanic population substantially above the 40 million mark by the turn of the century is not an unrealistic projection.

The millions of Hispanics living in the United States at the turn of the century will be speaking Spanish. There is no reason whatsoever to expect the U.S. Hispanic population suddenly to develop a preference for the English language, not when it has so stubbornly retained use of Spanish in the past. Third-, fourth-, and tenth-generation Hispanic families in the southwest are still speaking Spanish. Young Hispanic adults in Miami who came from Cuba when they were 2 or 3 years old speak both Spanish and English. Hispanic children born in the northeast or the midwest hear many of their first words in Spanish and grow up bilingual.

Hispanic participation in American society will become more notable and significant, particularly in areas of high Hispanic concentration. Candidates for political office will increasingly take the Hispanic vote into account as an important factor. Hispanic entrepreneurs and Hispanic business activity will be more in evidence.

The expected rise in Hispanic participation, however, does not mean that Hispanics will suddenly show an interest in assimilating, not when the ties to culture have been so demonstrably enduring and not when Hispanics continue to make strides in participation without having to trade in their cultural identity.

The pride that Hispanics have expressed in their heritage indicates that they will retain predictable behavior patterns directly related to the Hispanic culture—close family ties, respect for elders, strong sex role definition, adherence to Catholic beliefs, and, naturally, Spanish language use.

As the Hispanic population grows in size and economic power, so will Hispanic-oriented media grow in number and importance as advertising vehicles. Currently, U.S. Hispanics are a secondary audience for most of the media content available to them, be it an English language situation comedy produced for the general audience or a Spanish language *novela* produced for the Mexican audience in Mexico. While the cultural and language differences between a U.S. Hispanic and a Mexican in Mexico City may not be as striking as the differences between a U.S. Hispanic and a non-Hispanic American, differences certainly exist that influence media content preferences.

For essentially economic reasons, the U.S. Hispanic population remains largely unapproached as a primary audience, even as Spanish media continue to develop in the United States and some material is produced with U.S. Hispanics as the primary audience. For essentially economic reasons, U.S. Hispanics will be recognized as a primary audience to a much greater extent in the future.

The projected growth of the U.S. Hispanic population has already been noted. Concurrently with growing awareness of the Hispanic market potential, the economic connection between programming originators and programming consumers is becoming increasingly direct. This connection is facilitated by the growing use and capabilities of cable television, subfrequencies, satellites, earth stations, translators, etc., to deliver high-interest programming to a select and selective audience. The more directly a consumer can influence the choice of programming offered—as, for example, by the effect of purchase decisions for various pay-television services—the more profitable it becomes for a programmer to serve relatively small but intensely interested audiences with special material.

Today, the Hispanic population is already an attractive market for programmers and one whose commercial value will continue to grow. The potential for profit can be expected to draw increasing investments of talent, money, and resources into the development and delivery of media services designed for the special interests of the U.S. Hispanic audience. The tangible results of this expected investment—media content designed with U.S. Hispanics as the primary audience—is already in evidence and will continue to develop.

To the advertisers, this development will mean a great increase in the number and types of vehicles that they will have at their command to reach the U.S. Hispanic market and to reach the specific segment of the Hispanic market in which they are most interested. In print, more Spanish language magazines will appear that will focus on special interests. The number of bilingual and English language magazines aimed at Hispanics will also increase, particularly magazines aimed at a young Hispanic readership educated in the United States.

Because of their larger numbers, Spanish radio stations will increasingly concentrate on attracting a narrowly defined segment of the total Hispanic audience. There will be a greater variety of Spanish language radio formats as stations experiment with talk and all-news formats, among others. Some Spanish music stations will feature a playlist blending popular Hispanic and American songs in order to appeal to the young bilingual Hispanic. In multinationality Hispanic markets, Spanish radio stations will design their formats to attract one specific Spanish-origin group. U.S. Hispanic artists and songs will gain greater air play as their popularity grows. Non-Hispanic Americans will begin to produce bilingual and Spanish language versions of songs with the U.S. Hispanic market in mind.

Spanish television will see a substantial growth in domestically produced Hispanic programs. English language independent stations in areas of high Hispanic concentration will begin to devote larger segments of their broadcast day to Hispanic programming. Hispanic syndicated programming particularly will grow. Domestic producers will experiment with bilingual and English language programs aimed at specific segments of the Hispanic market. Cable systems will carry at least one Spanish language channel. The number of Spanish-television programming imports will rise owing to increased demand for quantity.

Hispanic-audience ratings surveys conducted by services other than Nielsen and Arbitron will be more widely accepted by broadcasters and advertisers alike. Nielsen and Arbitron will undertake more intensive efforts and will experiment with new methodologies designed to measure accurately Hispanic radio and television audiences.

As the U.S. Hispanic market and Spanish media grow, so will Hispanic advertising. Assigning part of the overall advertising budget to Hispanic advertising will become common practice for products with a high consumption index in the Hispanic market. All major general-market advertising agencies will begin to offer Hispanic advertising services. Independent Hispanic advertising agencies will grow dramatically in number and billings.

Advertising competition for the Hispanic consumer will increase tremendously. The same opportunity that exists today for the advertiser to dominate share of voice in a product category with a limited investment will not be available to the same degree 5 or 10 years from now. Brands that entered the Hispanic market early and sustained their advertising levels will enjoy a large share of the Hispanic market.

Because of increased Hispanic advertising competition, the development of the Hispanic campaign will receive greater attention. The creative strategy will become particularly important. Hispanic creative strategies will center on what will work for the specific Hispanic market segment that the advertiser is pursuing rather than what will work for the Hispanic market as a whole. Hispanic adaptations of general-market campaigns will become less common. The practice of dubbing an English language commercial into Spanish, particularly, will decrease.

Bilingual Hispanic advertising will become more important, especially as a way of reaching young Hispanics. English language commercials will also be developed with a bilingual Hispanic target audience in mind. Spanish language Hispanic advertising, however, will retain its position of prominence as the most effective way to reach the Hispanic market.

Bibliography

Articles

"Advertisers Hesitant to Approach Hispanic Market," *Adweek*. Mar. 31, 1980.

"Advertising's Missed Opportunity: The Hispanic Market," *Marketing and Media Decisions*. January 1980.

Aguayo, Joseph M. "Latinos: Los que importan son ustedes," *Sales and Marketing Management*. July 11, 1977.

"Along the Mexican Border—A New Era of Friendship," *U.S. News & World Report*. Nov. 30, 1964, pp. 75–78.

Alzaga, Florinda. "The Three Roots of Cuban Heritage," *Agenda*. January/February 1980, pp. 22–27.

Anselmo, Rene. "Hispanic Television in the 1980's," *Hispanic Business*. October 1980, p. 8.

Anson, Roberto. "Hispanics in the United States: Yesterday, Today, and Tomorrow," *The Futurist*. August 1980, pp. 25–31.

Auerbach, Alexander. "Hispanic Market? Si! Same Old Methods? No!" *Marketing Times*. July/August 1977, pp. 5–8.

Banas, Casey, and Meg O'Connor. "Latinos Exceed Whites in City's Grade Schools," *Chicago Tribune*. Dec. 20, 1980.

Bell, Clark W. "JWT says 'Si' to Hispanic Market," *Chicago Sun-Times*. Sept. 17, 1980.

Benton, Pat Moran. "Hispanics and the Census: A Chance To Be Counted," *The Arizona Daily Star*. Dec. 16, 1979.

Berman, Phyllis. "Does the Melting Pot Still Meld?" *Forbes*. Oct. 30, 1978, pp. 63–67.

"The Bilingual Quandry," *Californian*. Sept. 11, 1979.

Blum, Howard. "Illegal Aliens in New York: A Life of Fear, Costly to All," *The New York Times*. Mar. 18, 1979.

Blum, Howard. "Illegal Aliens Cause Loss of Millions in Aid to City," *The New York Times*. Mar. 19, 1979.

"Border Boom," *Time*. Jan. 8, 1979, pp. 46–47.

Brenner, Elizabeth. "12 Million Consumers Ignored due Mainly to Language," *The Houston Post*. Aug. 12, 1979.

Brown, Hal. "Latin 'Stranger in His Own Land,' " *The Times* (Corpus Christi). Sept. 10, 1979.

Burkholtz, Herbert. "The Latinization of Miami," *The New York Times Magazine*. Sept. 21, 1980.

Caballero, Eduardo. "Have You Looked at the Huge Spanish-Speaking Market Lately?" *Minority Advertising*. Autumn 1978, pp. 18–20, 23.

Campos, Leonel. "El Descubrimiento de América," *La Raza* (Chicago). Oct. 15–21, 1980, pp. 13, 22.

Cantu, Felipe. "Reaching Hispanics," *Adweek*. Mar. 17, 1980.

"Chicanos on the Move," *Newsweek*. Jan. 1, 1979, pp. 22–26.

"City Maintains that Census 'Undercounts' Illegal Aliens," *The New York Times*. Mar. 19, 1979.

Coakley, Michael. "Latino Progress Slow in Chicago," *Chicago Tribune*. May 25, 1979.

Coile, Norma. "Brewer Toasts Hispanic Decade," *Sun & Sentinel* (Yuma, Ariz.). Jan. 7, 1980.

Collins, Chris. "Advertisers Urged to Aim for Hispanics," *Tucson Daily Citizen*. Nov. 28, 1980.

"Colorado's Hispanic Heritage," *Empire—Denver Post Sunday Magazine*. Nov. 25, 1979.

"Coors Seeking Spanish Language Beer Drinkers," *Valley News and Tribune* (Gardena, Calif.). Dec. 20, 1979.

Cortes, Carlos C. "The Chicanos—A Frontier People," *Agenda*. January/February 1980, pp. 16–21, 42.

Crewdson, John M. "Border Region Is Almost a Country unto Itself, neither Mexican nor American," *The New York Times*. Feb. 14, 1979.

Crewdson, John M. "Hispanic Influx Moving U.S. Closer to Bilingualism," *The New York Times*. Aug. 8, 1979.

Cruz, Amaury. "The Cubans: What Kind of Welcome is This?" *Nuestro*. August 1980, pp. 57–59, 62.

Dart, Bob. "Latinization of America: Big Bird to Grande Mac," *The Miami News*. Feb. 27, 1979.

Dickstein, George. "Spanish-Language Market," *Television/Radio Age*. Sept. 29, 1975.

"Differences Shown in Black, Hispanic Overall TV Ratings," *Television/Radio Age*. Nov. 5, 1979, p. 127.

Downing, Margaret. "Millions Flow from Texas Yearly," *Dallas Time Herald.* June 2, 1979.

Du Brow, Rick. "Spanish-Language Stations Boom in '80s," *Herald Examiner* (Los Angeles). July 30, 1980.

Easterbrook, Gregg. "English, Si. Spanish, No," *The Washington Monthly.* December 1980, pp. 37–44.

Elliott, Stuart. "Spanish-Language Ads Translate into Big Dollars," *Mercury* (San Jose). June 18, 1980.

Erickson, Richard. "A Hispanic Touch in Advertising," *San Antonio Express-News.* June 1, 1980.

Espinal, Antonio. "Tres millones de Hispanos en Nueva York," *Temas.* October 1978, pp. 30–31.

"Ethnic Markets Worth Reaching," *Adbiz,* December 1979, p. 8.

"Feeling for the Spanish-Speaking Population," *Minority Advertising.* Autumn 1978, pp. 12, 14.

Fernández, Fernando J. "Día de La Raza: Día de los Hispanos en EE. UU.," *La Raza* (Chicago). Oct. 15–21, 1980, pp. 8, 10, 12.

Finder, Harvey. "Many Markets, Many Strategies," *Anny.* July 9, 1979, pp. 30, 46, 50, 60.

Flynn, Ken. "Cultural Bridges," *El Paso Herald Post.* June 2, 1979.

Forkan, James P. "Big, Booming—and Still Neglected," *Advertising Age.* Apr. 16, 1979, pp. S-2, S-4, S-6, S-8, S-10, S-12, S-14.

Galleguillos, Oreste. "El Censo de 1980 y la participación de los indocumentados," *El Sol De Texas.* Feb. 15, 1980.

García Mazas, José. "Reflecting on Language," *Agenda.* May/June 1980, pp. 22–29, 53–54.

Garvin, Glenn, and Bob Dart. "Frito Bandido Is Dead; Viva Chicanos," *The Miami News.* Feb. 27, 1979.

Godsell, Geoffrey. "Hispanics in the US: Ethnic 'Sleeping Giant' Awakens," *The Christian Science Monitor.* Apr. 28, 1980, p. 3.

Godsell, Geoffrey. "The Chicanos," *The Christian Science Monitor.* Apr. 29, 1980, pp. 11–13.

Godsell, Geoffrey. "The Cubans," *The Christian Science Monitor.* Apr. 30, 1980, pp. 11–13.

Godsell, Geoffrey. "The Puerto Ricans," *The Christian Science Monitor.* May 1, 1980, pp. 11–13.

Godsell, Geoffrey. "Hispanics—The Challenge Ahead," *The Christian Science Monitor.* May 2, 1980, pp. 12–13.

Goldin, Elyse. "Hispanic Population Expected to Grow at Fast Rate in U.S., Census Official Says," *State News* (Michigan State University, East Lansing). Apr. 16, 1980.

Gonzalez, Raymond J. "Hispanics Move into the 80's," *Caminos*. March 1980, pp. 14–17, 42.

Green, Wayne E. "Reaching Out," *The Wall Street Journal*. Nov. 10, 1980.

Grove, Lloyd. "Channel 56," *The Washington Post*. July 1980.

"The Growing Hispanic Presence," *Commerce* (Chicago). March 1980, pp. 96, 98, 122.

Guernica, Antonio. "The Public Airwaves: Who Owns Them?" *Agenda*. March/April 1977, pp. 39–40, 42.

Guernica, Antonio. "Cable Television . . . The Medium for Hispanics?" *Agenda*. May/June 1977, pp. 25–27.

Guernica, Antonio. "Las Realidades de Raquel Ortiz, An Interview with a Latina Television Producer," *Agenda*. July/August 1977, pp. 40–41.

Guernica, Antonio. "Nielsen, Arbitron and Spanish Audience Ratings—Special Report," *NASB News/Noticias*, National Association of Spanish Broadcasters. October 1979.

Gutierrez, Felix F. "Latino Media: An Historical Overview," *Nuestro*. October 1980, pp. 25–28.

Gutierrez, Felix, and Jorge Reina Schement. "Chicanos and the Media: A Bibliography of Selected Materials," *Journalism History*. Summer 1977.

Gutierrez, Ivan. "El Canal 41 y su Nueva Victoria," *Noticias del Mundo*. June 8, 1980, p. 13.

Halleen, Valerie. "The Illegal Alien Problem," *Orange Coast*. February 1980, pp. 95–100.

Halsell, Grace. "The Melting Pot's Mexican Roots," *The New York Times*. July 25, 1978.

Hansen, Charles J. "Expanded Role Seen for Hispanics," *Lowry Airman* (Denver). Sept. 12, 1980.

Harris, Michael. "Toward a New Ethnic Majority," *Californian*. September 1978, pp. 71–72, 74.

Held, Robert. "The Latinization of America," *World Press Review*. November 1980.

Henry, Diane. "For State's Hispanics, Hope and Frustration," *The New York Times*. May 25, 1980.

Herbers, John. "Census Bureau Bars Shift in '80 Figures," *The New York Times*. Dec. 11, 1980.

Hernández, Al Carlos. "Spanish-Language Radio: Time to Tune In Quality," *Nuestro*. October 1980, p. 54.

"Hispanic Advertising More Than Just Spanish Voiceovers," *Adweek*. Sept. 22, 1980, p. 21.

"Hispanic Americans, Soon: The Biggest Minority," *Time*. Oct. 16, 1978, pp. 48–52, 55, 58, 61.

"The Hispanic Broadcast Focus," *Television/Radio Age.* (series of articles). Dec. 15, 1980.

"Hispanic Business Ownership Up 53%: Nationwide Survey," *Journal of Commerce Review.* Sept. 19, 1980.

"Hispanic Celebrities on TV Aid Census," *The New York Times.* Mar. 8, 1980.

"Hispanic Community Can No Longer Be Ignored," *The Muskegon Chronicle.* July 20, 1979.

"The Hispanic Decade," *Television/Radio Age.* (series of articles). Dec. 10, 1979.

"Hispanic Firms on Increase," *Belvedere Citizen.* Sept. 10, 1980.

"Hispanic Marketing," *Advertising Age.* Section 2. (series of articles). Apr. 6, 1981, pp. S1–S24.

"Hispanic Market's Sharp Growth is Altering Some U.S. Marketing Tactics," *The Wall Street Journal.* Oct. 18, 1979.

"Hispanic Population Will Be Major Concern in 1980 Census," *Sun-Herald.* Nov. 22, 1979.

" 'Hispanic power'—An Elusive Goal," *Chicago Tribune.* May 21, 1979.

" 'Hispanic Power': Challenge for American Catholicism," *Chicago Tribune.* May 24, 1979.

"Hispanics Are Huge Market That's Neglected," *Chicago Tribune.* July 20, 1979.

"Hispanics: Forward with Pride," *Nevada State Journal Gazette.* Nov. 9, 1980.

"Hispanic Slight by Television," *Michigan Chronicle.* Nov. 24, 1979.

"Hispanics Offer Opportunity for Increased Sales," *Modern Grocer,* Apr. 4, 1980.

"Hispanics Push for Bigger Role in Washington," *U.S. News & World Report.* May 22, 1978, pp. 58, 61.

Howard-Jones, Marje. "Latin Pride: 'We're Like a Nation within a Nation,' " *Journal* (Carlsbad, Calif.). June 7, 1980.

"How Campbell's Got a Spanish Accent," *Marketing & Media Decisions.* November 1979.

"How the Immigrants Made It in Miami," *Business Week.* May 1, 1971, pp. 88–89.

"Immigration: Still They Come," *Forbes.* Oct. 30, 1978, pp. 63–67.

"In Mexico, There Is No Life for Me. Here I Want Only a Chance To Work and Live," *Atlanta.* November 1980.

Irizarry, Estelle. "Reflecting on Culture," *Agenda.* July/August 1980, pp. 22–27, 38, 47.

Jarboe, Jan. "Politicians and Hispanic TV," *The Light* (San Antonio). Nov. 24, 1980.

Jarboe, Jan. "The Special Case of Spanish-Language Television," *Washington Journalism Review.* November 1980, pp. 21–23, 25.

"Johnston's Aims Yogurts at Hispanics," *Advertising Age.* Jan. 22, 1979.

Jordan, Phil. "Our Hispanic Future," *El Chicano* (Colton, Calif.). Aug. 14, 1980.

Jory, Tom. "Spanish TV Network Broadens Horizons," *Asbury Park Press.* Oct. 5, 1979.

Jory, Tom. "Spanish Network Pushes Census," *Today's Spirit.* Feb. 15, 1980.

Kelley, Daryl. "The 'Invisible' Minority Is Breaking Its Silence," *Nevada State Journal Gazette.* Apr. 22, 1979.

Kelley, William. "The Voice That Speaks to Hispanic Americans," *Broadcast Daily.* Apr. 14, 1981.

Kirsch, Jonathan. "Chicano Power," *New West.* Sept. 11, 1978, pp. 35–40.

Klain, Stephen. "Aim at Broader Marketing Ploy," *Variety.* May 28, 1980, pp. 3, 41.

Koris, Sally. "Se habla Espanol: It Means M-O-N-E-Y," *Herald Examiner* (Los Angeles). Dec. 31, 1979.

Kowet, Don. "The Wages of SIN," *TV Guide.* Dec. 15–21, 1979.

"L.A. Hispanics Favor U.S.–Made Automobiles," *Adweek.* Oct. 13, 1980.

Langley, Roger. "Republicans Seek To Build upon Hispanic Voting Gains," *The Courier-News.* Oct. 12, 1979.

Langley, Roger. "By 1990 U.S. Will Be Second Largest Hispanic Country," *Times* (Marietta, Ohio). Dec. 12, 1979.

Langley, Roger. "Hispanic America—Census May Miss—Again," *Californian.* Apr. 2, 1980.

Langley, Roger. "The Hispanic Market," *Hispanic Affairs* (Port Huron, Mich.). Oct. 5, 1980.

Langley, Roger. "Hispanic Market Fastest Growing in U.S.," *Niagara Falls Gazette.* Nov. 30, 1980.

Lanier, Alfredo S. "Giant Latino Market Inspires New Businesses," *Crain's Chicago Business.* July 10, 1978.

"La Saguesera: Miami's Little Havana," *Time.* Oct. 14, 1974, p. 24.

"Latino Businesses Planting Stronger Roots in Midlands," *Omaha World-Herald.* Sept. 9, 1979.

"Latinos in U.S.: 'Our Muscle Is Just Starting To Be Felt,' " *U.S. News & World Report.* Dec. 13, 1976, p. 56.

"Latins Are Fastest-Growing U.S. Minority," *Courier-Times* (New Castle, Ind.). Oct. 30, 1979.

Lindsey, Robert. "Hispanics' Influence on Los Angeles Grows," *The New York Times.* Feb. 20, 1978.

Lindsey, Robert. "Hispanic Minority Fastest-Growing in U.S.," *The New York Times.* Feb. 18, 1979.

Lindsey, Robert. "Los Angeles, Almost 200 Rank No. 2 among Cities," *The New York Times.* Sept. 8, 1980.

López, Alfredo. "By 1990, the No. 1 Minority," *The Record* (Hackensack, N.J.). Oct. 9, 1979.

López, Enrique Hank. "When the Census Man Gets to the Barrio, He May Discover the Numbers Aren't There," *Herald Examiner* (Los Angeles). Apr. 1, 1980.

Lozano, Anthony G. "Tracing the Spanish Language," *Agenda*. March/April 1980, pp. 32–39.

MacDonald, Marcia. "Up for the Count Hispanics: The Invisible Americans," *TVC* (Englewood, Calif.). May 15, 1980, pp. 158–159.

Maeroff, Gene I. "Hispanic Enrollment Surges against the Tide," *The New York Times*. Nov. 18, 1980.

"Marketing Skill—and Art—Builds $40 Million Hispanic Food Sales," *Food Promotions*. June 1980.

Martínez, Ron. "Hispanos Aim for Advance in the '80s," *Star Journal* (Pueblo, Colo.). Jan. 14, 1980.

Massing, Michael, "America Discovers Its Hispanic Consumers," *Marketing Communications*. March-April 1978, pp. 29–31.

Maxwell, Evan. "Latino Cooperation with Census Exceeds Forecast," *Los Angeles Times*. Apr. 16, 1980.

McArthur, Edith. "How Wide is the Language Gap?" *American Demographics*. May 1981, pp. 28–33.

McCarron, John. "Chicago's Latinos Find Selves in 'Ethnic Trap,' " *Chicago Tribune*. May 19, 1977.

McCormack, Patricia. "¿Habla usted Español? If Not . . . Watch Out!" *San Antonio Light*. July 9, 1980.

McElmurry, Michel. "Hispanics and Media Discuss Stereotypes," *State News* (Michigan State University). June 25, 1979.

McMahan, Harry Wayne. "Mexican Commercials Show Quality on Moderate Budgets," *Advertising Age*. May 9, 1977.

Medina, David. "Hispanic News a Low Priority," *Adweek*. May 26, 1980.

Medina, David. "Another Special Case: Spanish-Language Newspapers," *Washington Journalism Review*. November 1980.

Mendoza, Carlos J. "Sobre un periodismo etnico," *La Raza* (Chicago). Oct. 15–21, 1980, p. 14.

Mendoza, Rick. "Programming Galavision," *Hispanic Business*. October 1980, pp. 16–17.

"Mex America," *The Washington Post*. (series of articles). Mar. 26–30, 1978.

"Mexican Guest Worker Plan Could End Chaos," *News-Sentinel* (Lodi, Calif.). July 7, 1980.

"Mexican Shopper Totals ½ Billion," *Star News* (Chula Vista, Calif.). Mar. 25, 1979.

"Mexican Travelers Spent 17 Percent More in 1979," *International*. Mar. 28, 1980.

Meyer, Richard E. "Minorities Take Over This Year as Majority," *Los Angeles Times*. Apr. 13, 1980.

"Miami: Latin Crossroads," *Newsweek*. Feb. 11, 1980.

Middleton, Lorenzo. "Hispanics on the Campuses: A Long Way To Go," *The Chronicle of Higher Education*. June 2, 1980.

"Minorities in Labor Force Said Increasing," *El Paso Herald-Post*. Dec. 2, 1977.

Molina, Mauricio. "America is the Land of Opportunity—for Hispanics To Learn English," *San Jose Mercury*. June 6, 1980.

Molina, Mauricio. "Why Spanish Translations?!" *The Saturday Evening Post*. July/August 1980.

Montemayor, Robert. "Illegal Aliens' Wages Put at $150 Million," *Los Angeles Times*. Mar. 26, 1980.

Morales-Carrión, Arturo. "Reflecting on Common Hispanic Roots," *Agenda*. March/April 1980, pp. 28–30.

Naunton, Ene. "Latin Power—Call to Unity Grew from Past of Poverty," *The Miami Herald*. Feb. 23, 1980.

Navarro, Mireya. "A Hard Look/Hispanics a Special Challenge for Advertisers," *San Francisco Examiner*. Feb. 24, 1981.

"The New Immigrants," *Newsweek*. July 7, 1980, pp. 26–31.

"1980 Census Population Totals for Racial and Spanish Origin Groups in U.S. Announced by Census Bureau," *U.S. Department of Commerce News*. Feb. 23, 1981.

Ojeda, Tony. "Miami Meets Challenge of Cuban Influx," *Californian*. June 12, 1980.

"O'Mara, Susana H. "The Hispanic Presence," *The Sun* (Baltimore). Nov. 8, 1979.

"Ore-Ida Gears to Hispanics," *MAC* (Los Angeles). Jan. 1, 1980.

Pearce, Carol A. "U.S. Ethnic Market," *Back Stage*. June 29, 1979.

Peirce, Neal R. "It's Hispanics' Turn at U.S. City Gates," *The San Diego Union*. May 6, 1979.

Peirce, Neal R. "Journalism Meets Hispanics' Needs," *The Detroit News*. May 20, 1979.

Pérez-Luna, Elizabeth. "Public TV and Latinos: No Medium No Message," *Nuestro*. October 1980, pp. 34–36.

Peterson, Bill. "Miami—The New 'Capital' of Latin America," *San Francisco Examiner*. Dec. 17, 1978.

Pineda, Hugo. "The Hispanic Character," *Agenda*. July/August 1980, pp. 28–33, 47.

Pino, Frank, Jr. "The 'Great' Cultural Tradition of Hispanics," *Agenda*. May/June, 1980, pp. 38–43.

Pope, Leroy. "Latino Market Fastest Growing," *The Atlanta Journal and Constitution*. Aug. 7, 1977.

"The Pot Still Simmers," *Review* (Reidsville, N.C.). Aug. 30, 1979.

Pritchard, Rev. David G. "Reaching into the Hispanic Community," *The Living Church* (Milwaukee, Wis.). July 22, 1979, pp. 8–11.

"Proud To Be a Hispanic," *The News World* (special edition). (series of articles). Dec. 14–16, 1979.

Psaltis, Mike. "The Hispanic Market: Large and Largely Untapped," *Madison Avenue*. August 1980.

Raven, Margot. "The Spanish-Speaking Market: Big, Growing, and Spending," *Drug Topics*. July 1980.

"Reaching the Hispanic Market," *Boardroom Reports*. Dec. 15, 1979.

Reeves, Richard. "Mexican America," *Esquire*. Jan. 2, 1979.

Reinhold, Robert. "Should Census Count the Illegal Alien?" *The New York Times*. Feb. 7, 1980.

Rendón, Armando B. "Será fácil responder al censo a la mayoría de los Norteamericanos," *Diario Las Americas*. Feb. 12, 1980.

Rendón, Armando B. "Buscan ayuda local para el censo," *Diario Las Americas*. Feb. 16, 1980.

Revett, John. "GM Joins Swing to Latin-Oriented Campaigns," *Advertising Age*. May 23, 1977.

"Revival of Ethnicity in Advertising is Spreading to Include Hispanics," *Arkansas Gazette*. June 1, 1980.

Rodríguez, Eliott, and Ana Veciana. "Heavy Latin Vote Sways Miami, Hialeah Races," *The Miami News*. Nov. 7, 1979.

Rodríguez, Ray M. "Will Spanish Ads Sway Next Election?" *Marketing & Media Decisions*. September 1979.

Romo, Carlos, and Michael Passi. "80's—Decade of New Life for Hispanics," *Nevada State Journal Gazette*. Sept. 9, 1979.

Rule, Sheila. "Hispanic-Americans Live with Diversity of Cultures," *The New York Times*. Nov. 22, 1977.

Rusher, William. "Our Hispanic 'Quebec'?" *Nashville Banner*. June 4, 1979.

Russell, John A., "Hispanic Market Holds Promise," *Automotive News*, May 7, 1979.

Sales, Miguel. "Cuando los cubanos se fueron," *El Miami Herald*. July 1, 1980.

"San José: This Cultural Blender Serves the Unique Fare," *South San José Sun*. May 2, 1979.

Sawyer, Susan G. "Puerto Rican Women: New Strength, New Determination," *Daily News*. Nov. 9, 1979.

Schement, Jorge Reina. "Who Owns Spanish Language Radio?" *Agenda.* September/October 1977, pp. 26–28.

Schement, Jorge Reina, and Ricardo Flores. "The Origins of Spanish-Language Radio: The Case of San Antonio, Texas," *Journalism History,* vol. 4, no. 2, Summer 1977.

Schonbak, Judith. "New Patterns, New People," *Atlanta.* November 1980, pp. 125, 127–128, 131–132, 175.

Seamans, Ike. "Miami Dances to a Latin Beat," *The San Diego Union.* Feb. 4, 1979.

Slayman, E. J., and Deborah Weser. "People Equal Dollars—So Census Is Interesting," *The Light* (San Antonio). Nov. 25, 1979.

Sosa, Lionel. "Spanish Market? ¡Si! ¡Si!" *Adweek.* Nov. 12, 1979.

Sosa, Lionel. "The Spanish Language Market in Simple English," *Adweek.* Dec. 10, 1979.

Sosa, Lionel. "Reach Hispanic Sub-segments through Generic Advertising," *Adweek.* Mar. 24, 1980.

"Spanish is Número Dos in U.S. Today," *The Miami News.* Aug. 8, 1979.

"Spanish Language Expertise Pulling Clients," *Southern Advertising/Markets.* March/April 1978.

"Spanish-Language Market Study," *Television/Radio Age.* (series of articles). Nov. 7, 1977.

"Spanish-Language Market Study," *Television/Radio Age.* (series of articles). Oct. 23, 1978.

"Spanish-Language Stations Seen Increasing Rapidly," *Television/Radio Age.* Dec. 1, 1980.

"Spanish Soon Will Be Second Language," *Olympian.* (Olympia, Wash.). Oct. 5, 1979.

"Special Background Report on Trends in Industry and Finance, Business Bulletin," *The Wall Street Journal.* July 28, 1977.

"Special TV Networks for Special Audiences," *The New York Times.* Apr. 8, 1980.

Spielberg Benítez, José. "The 'Little' Cultural Tradition of Hispanics," *Agenda.* May/June 1980, pp. 30–37, 53.

"The State of the Art," *Texas Business.* April 1980.

Stevens, William K. "Millions of Mexicans View Illegal Entry to U.S. as Door to Opportunity," *The New York Times.* Feb. 12, 1979.

Stevens, William K. "San Antonio, with Mexican-Americans in Power, Is at a Crossroad," *The New York Times.* Apr. 7, 1979.

Stiteler, Betsy. "Hispanics: A New Market," *The Dallas Morning News.* Dec. 2, 1980.

"Studying the Diocesan Census: III—Hispanics," *Western N.Y. Catholic Visitor.* Apr. 27, 1980.

"Tapping the Elusive U.S. Hispanic Market," *Adweek.* Apr. 14, 1980.

"Targeting the Black/Hispanic Markets," *Ad Forum.* September 1980, pp. 23–26.

Tasker, Frederick. "Citan gran alza demográfica en Dade," *El Miami Herald.* Aug. 21, 1980.

"This One Counts," *The Miami News.* Feb. 19, 1980.

Thurow, Lester C. "Hispanics Continuing Economic Gains," *Morning Advocate* (Baton Rouge). June 3, 1979.

Treviño, Jesús Salvador, and José Luis Ruiz, "A History of Neglect," *The Independent* (New York). October 1979, pp. 12–15.

Trujillo, Ignacio. "El Censo," *Argus* (Fremont, Calif.). Mar. 27, 1980.

"Trying to Tap the Huge Hispanic Market," *Texas Business.* April 1980.

"A Uniquely American Paradox," *Forbes.* Oct. 30, 1978, pp. 69–75.

de Uriarte, Mercedes Lynn. " 'Invisible' Market Too Often Ignored," *Advertising Age.* Mar. 26, 1979.

Valente, Judith. "Special School Opens to Meet Needs of Hispanic Teen-Agers," *The Washington Post.* Feb. 4, 1980.

Vazquez, Francisco. "The Farm-Worker Struggle: A Historical Drama & Lesson," *Caminos.* March 1980, pp. 32–33, 47.

Verdon, Joan. "Hispanic Aim Is To Send More Students to College," *The Grand Rapids Press.* May 12, 1980.

Vidal, David. "For Hispanic Migrants 'Home' Is Elusive," *The New York Times.* May 19, 1980.

Vidal, David. "Hispanic Newcomers in City Cling to Values of Homeland," *The New York Times.* May 11–14, 1980.

Vivó, Paquita, "The Puerto Ricans—Two Communities, One Culture," *Agenda.* January/February 1980, pp. 28–31.

Volsky, George. "Non-Cuban Latinos in Miami Growing in Economic Impact," *The New York Times.* Mar. 5, 1979.

Walker, Jean. "Miami's Hispanic Revolution: Anglo Advertisers Find Token Budgets Are Not Enough Anymore," *Adweek.* Aug. 11, 1980, pp. 14, 16.

Weiner, Rochelle. "Spanish-Language Market," *Television/Radio Age.* Oct. 23, 1978.

"Why 10,000 Cubans Grab Chance to Leave," *U.S. News & World Report.* Apr. 21, 1980, p. 13.

Williams, Dan. "Madison Avenue Touts Latin Market," *The Miami Herald.* Sept. 6, 1980.

Wolin, Merle Linda. "L.A.'s 'Nation Unto Itself' Casts Spell on Retailers, Advertisers," *Herald Examiner* (Los Angeles). Apr. 1, 1980.

Wolin, Merle Linda, "Who's Buying the Fruit Juice in L.A.?" *Herald Examiner* (Los Angeles). Sept. 26, 1980.

"Working the Hispanic Market," *Hispanic Business.* November 1979.

"Y&R Ethnic Unit: Finding and Reaching Minority Markets—Monday Memo," *Broadcasting.* June 4, 1973.

Zubizarreta, Teri A. "Assimilation Far from Real in Hispanic Community," *Advertising Age.* Apr. 16. 1979.

Books and Reports

The Arbitron Company. *How Blacks and Spanish Listen to Radio.* Reports 1–4. 1975, 1976, 1977, 1978.

The Arbitron Company. *Measuring the Hispanic Radio Audience—A Report on the Hispanic Ethnic Procedures Study from Arbitron Research.* September 1979.

Audience Profile Services. *A Literature Review and Analysis of Radio Ratings Methods with Emphasis on Minority Measurement.* Feb. 17, 1981. (Submitted to National Telecommunications Information Agency.)

Bran, M. M. *Island in the Crossroads.* Doubleday, New York. 1968.

Craig, Richard B. *The Bracero Program.* University of Texas Press, Austin. 1971.

Cuantos somos: A Demographic Study of the Mexican American Population. Center for Mexican Studies, The University of Texas, Austin. 1977.

Dinnerstein, Leonard, and David M. Reimers. *Ethnic Americans.* Dodd, Mead & Company, New York. 1975.

The Gallup Organization. *Hispanic Media Preference for Music and Entertainment.* October 1980. (Conducted for Caballero Spanish Media.)

The Gallup Organization. *Listening and Viewing Habits of Hispanic Americans.* September 1979. (Conducted for Caballero Spanish Media.)

Greenberg, Bradley S., Carrie Heeter, David Graef, and Kurt Doctor. *Mass Communication and Hispanic Americans.* Department of Communication, Michigan State University. 1980.

Guernica, Antonio. *Ratings—Field Study Design Group.* National Association of Spanish Broadcasters. 1980. (unpublished report.)

Guernica, Antonio (ed.). *The United States Hispanic Market—1980.* National Association of Spanish Broadcasters and Strategy Research Corporation. 1980.

Guernica, Antonio (ed.). *U.S. Hispanics—A Market Profile.* National Association of Spanish Broadcasters and Strategy Research Corporation. 1980.

Roslow, Peter. "An Analysis of Spanish Radio Usage " (unpublished master's thesis, New York University). 1976.

Steiner, Stan. *La Raza—The Mexican Americans.* Harper & Row, New York. 1969.

Steiner, Stan. *The Islands.* Harper & Row, New York. 1974.

U.S. Bureau of the Census. Census of Population: 1970. *Subject Reports: Persons of Spanish Ancestry,* ser. PC(SI)-30. Issued 1973.

U.S. Bureau of the Census. Census of Population: 1970. *Subject Reports: Persons of Spanish Origin,* ser. PC(2)-1C. Issued 1973.

U.S. Bureau of the Census. Census of Population: 1970. *Subject Reports: Persons of Spanish Surname,* ser. PC(2)-1D. Issued 1973.

U.S. Bureau of the Census. Current Population Reports. *Subject Reports: Persons of Spanish Origin in the United States—March 1972 and 1971,* ser. P-20, no. 250. Issued 1973.

U.S. Bureau of the Census. Current Population Reports. *Subject Reports: Persons of Spanish Origin in the United States—March 1973,* ser. P-20, no. 264. Issued 1974.

U.S. Bureau of the Census. Current Population Reports. *Subject Reports: Persons of Spanish Origin in the United States—March 1974,* ser. P-20, no. 280. Issued 1975.

U.S. Bureau of the Census. Current Population Reports. *Subject Reports: Persons of Spanish Origin in the United States—March 1975,* ser. P-20, no. 290. Issued 1976.

U.S. Bureau of the Census. Current Population Reports. *Subject Reports: Persons of Spanish Origin in the United States—March 1976,* ser. P-20, no. 310. Issued 1977.

U.S. Bureau of the Census. Current Population Reports. *Subject Reports: Persons of Spanish Origin in the United States—March 1977,* ser. P-20, no. 329. Issued 1978.

U.S. Bureau of the Census. Current Population Reports. *Subject Reports: Persons of Spanish Origin in the United States—March 1978,* ser. P-20, no. 339. Issued 1979.

U.S. Commission on Civil Rights. *Puerto Ricans in the Continental United States: An Uncertain Future.* October 1976.

U.S. Commission on Civil Rights. *Window Dressing on the Set: Women and Minorities in Television.* August 1977.

Yankelovich, Skelly, and White. *Spanish USA—A Study of the Hispanic Market in the United States.* June 1981. (Conducted for SIN-National Spanish Television Network.)

Interviews

Anselmo, Rene, President, SIN–National Spanish Television Network, Aug. 17, 1981, New York City.

Barba, Carlos, President, WNJU-TV Broadcasting Corporation, Feb. 4, 1981, New York City.

Caballero, Eduardo, President, Caballero Spanish Media, Feb. 3, 1981, New York City.

Conill, Alicia, Executive Vice President, Conill Advertising Assoc., Inc., May 5, 1981, New York City.

Diaz-Albertini, Luis, President, SAMS, Inc., Feb. 4, 1981, New York City.

Dillon, Richard, President, Mendoza, Dillon & Asociados, Jan. 20, 1981, New York City.

Miyares, Marcelino, President, OMAR, Inc., Feb. 13, 1981, Chicago.

Murtagh, James, Business Manager, The Bravo Group/Young & Rubicam, Inc., June 2, 1981. Washington, D.C./New York City (telephone interview).

Zubizarreta, Teresa, President, Zubi Advertising Services, Feb. 20, 1981, Washington, D.C./Miami (telephone interview).

Index

ADIs (areas of dominant influence), 67–68,
    86, 142, 149
Advertisements (*see* Commercials)
Advertiser, 103–105, 117, 166
Advertising, Hispanic, 104–111, 123–124,
    167
    coordination with general campaign,
        131–133, 167
    national versus regional approach,
        133–136
    print, 12–13
    radio, 22–23, 141–142
    share of voice, 107–108, 154, 167
    television, 42–43, 141–142
    (*See also* Advertising campaign; Case
        histories, advertising; Commercials;
        Creative strategy; Media plan)
Advertising agency:
    general-market, 103–104, 109–111, 167
        Hispanic division in, 108–111
    Hispanic, 108–111, 137–138, 167
        independent, 110–111
        listings of, 117–122
        selection of, 108–111
Advertising budget, 105, 107, 109–110,
    134, 141–142, 167
    Scott Paper Company case history,
        160–161
    in test market, 111–112
Advertising campaign:
    general-market, 103–104, 107–108, 111,
        123, 131–133
        adaptation to Hispanic campaign,
            131–133, 167

Advertising campaign (*Cont.*):
    Hispanic, 104, 111–112, 117, 123–124,
        130, 139, 167
        coordination with general campaign,
            131–133
        effectiveness of, 106–108
        elements complimentary to, 136–138
        national versus regional approach,
            133–136
        test market, 111–116
        (*See also* Advertising, Hispanic)
Agency (*see* Advertising agency)
Arbitron Company, 147–153, 167
    diaries, 148–150
    differential survey treatments (DST),
        149–150
    personal placement and retrieval (PPR)
        technique, 149
    radio, reports on, 19–22
    (*See also* Media plan)
Area of origin, Hispanic population, 52, 70
    table, 52
Areas of dominant influence (*see* ADIs)
Arizona, 57–59, 74–76, 83
Assimilation, 6–7, 82–84, 125–127, 129,
    165
Audience:
    bilingual, English and Spanish, 6–7
    monolingual, Spanish, 6–7
    national versus regional approach,
        133–136
    segmentation, 3–7, 152, 165–167
    unduplicated (*see* Unduplicated
        audience)

Audience (*Cont*.):
  (*See also* Magazines, Spanish;
    Newspapers, Spanish; Radio,
    Spanish; Television, Spanish)
Audience measurement (*see* Media plan;
    Ratings; Reach and frequency)

Bodegas, 86, 137
  (*See also* Product distribution)
Border markets, 68–69, 142
Braceros, 77
Brand, product, 108, 129, 137, 154
  awareness of: performance in test market
    situations, 111–115
    Scott Paper Company case history,
      159–161
  distribution of, 137–138
  preference for, 85–86, 129
  share of market, 106–108, 112–115,
    141–142, 167
    performance in test market, 112–115
  (*See also* Product)
Broadcast media:
  English, 3–5, 7
    (*See also* Radio, English; Television,
      English)
  Spanish, 5–7, 141–142
    (*See also* Audience; Radio, Spanish;
      Television, Spanish)
Broadcast Spanish (*see* Generic Spanish)
Budget (*see* Advertising budget)
Buying habits, Hispanic:
  product consumption indices (*see*
    Consumer behavior)
  product consumption levels, 105–106

Caballero Spanish Media, 145–146
  sales offices, 145
Cable systems, 35, 143, 166–167
California, 54–55, 57–59, 74–76, 83
Campaign (*see* Advertising campaign)
Case histories, advertising:
  Scott Paper Company, 155–161
  test market, 107, 112–115
Catholic religion, 59, 73, 84, 124, 127–128,
  165
Census (*see* U.S. Bureau of the Census)
Central and South Americans in the United
  States, population size of, 52, 70–71, 99
Character portrayal in Hispanic advertising,
  130–131

Chicago, 52, 54–55, 71, 135
  Hispanic population makeup in, 116
  as a test market, 116
Colorado, 57–58, 75
Comedies, television, 38–39
Commercials, 107–108, 167
  adaptation from English to Spanish,
    131–133, 167
  character portrayal in, 130–131
  jingles, 132
  use of local personalities in, 145
  use of music in, 129, 132, 136, 139
  (*See also* Creative strategy)
Consumer behavior, Hispanic, 85–99
  Los Angeles consumption indices, 89–92
    cleaners and paper goods, table, 91
    foods and beverages, table, 90
    health and beauty aids, table, 91
    miscellaneous products, table, 92
  Miami consumption indices, 94–97
    cleaners and paper goods, table, 97
    foods and beverages, table, 95–96
    health and beauty aids, table, 96
    miscellaneous products, table, 97
  national product usage, 98–99
    cleaners and paper goods, table, 99
    foods and beverages, table, 98
    health and beauty aids, table, 98
  New York consumption indices, 87–89
    cleaners and paper goods, table, 88
    foods and beverages, table, 87
    health and beauty aids, table, 88
    miscellaneous products, table, 89
  San Antonio consumption indices,
    92–94
    cleaners and paper goods, table, 93
    foods and beverages, table, 92
    health and beauty aids, table, 93
    miscellaneous products, table, 94
Costs per thousand (CPMs), 141, 150
Country of origin (*see* Area of origin)
Coupons, 138, 146
CPMs (costs per thousand), 141, 150
Creative strategy, Hispanic advertising,
  123–139, 167
  attitudinal similarities among Hispanics,
    128–129
  Catholic religion, influence of, on
    Hispanics, 59, 124, 127–128, 165
  character portrayal, 130–131
  coordination with general and Hispanic
    campaigns, 131–133, 167
  coupons, 138

Creative strategy, Hispanic
advertising (*Cont.*):
differences among Hispanic groups, 124,
138–139
family ties among Hispanics, 124,
126–127, 165
Hispanics' role in American society, 6–7,
82–84, 125–129, 139, 163–165
language use in, 5–7, 124–127, 165
music in, 129, 132–133, 136, 139
national versus regional approach,
133–136
product distribution, 137–138
public relations, 136–137
Scott Paper Company case history,
158–159
sex roles, 130–131, 165
Cuba, 80–82
American interest in, 80–81
Castro regime, 81–82
"freedom flights," 82
independence movement in, 80
Mariel flotilla, 82, 94
Spanish-American War, 80
trade with the United States, 81
U.S. military rule in, 80–81
Cubans in the United Sates, 5, 82–83,
138–139
advertising for, 134–135
employment of, 64–66
geographic concentration of, 60–61, 71
household size of, 59
immigration to the United States, 81–83
income of, 60–61
listening habits of, 21
population size of, 52, 70
Cultural values, 59, 73, 83, 123–124,
127–129, 138–139
role in Spanish media, 5–7, 10–12,
17–18, 23, 36, 38–39, 42, 139
(*See also* Catholic religion; Family,
Hispanic; Language use)

De Armas Publications, 9–10, 147
listings, 13–15
sales offices, 147
(*See also* Magazines, Spanish)
Demographics, 49–71
area of origin, 52, 70
geographic concentration, 70–71
table, 52
educational level, 61–64, 70, 163–164

Demographics, educational
level (*Cont.*):
by age and type of Spanish origin,
61–62
table, 62
by sex, age, and type of Spanish
origin, 62–64
table, 63
employment, 64–66, 163–164
by sex, type of Spanish origin, and job
category, 64–66
table, 66
by type of Spanish origin and job
category, 64–65
table, 65
growth, 55–57, 70
1970 to 1980, 55, 70, 164–165
table, 55
1970 to 1980 by region, 56–57
table, 56
household size, 59, 70, 163
table, 59
income, 59–61, 70, 85, 163–164
by geographic region, 60–61
table, 61
of Hispanics versus U.S. total
population, 59–60, 70
by type of Spanish origin, 59–60
table, 60
metropolitan versus non metropolitan
residence, 66–67, 70, 163
table, 67
percentage of total population: by
geographic region, table, 57
by state, 57–59
table, 58
size, 49–51, 106
age and sex distribution: median age,
50–51, 70
table, 51
by region and state, 54–55, 70
map, 53
table, 54
top thirty Hispanic ADIs, 67–68
table, 67
U.S.–Mexico border markets, 68–69
table, 69
world rank, 50–51, 69–70
table, 51
Diaries, 148–150
(*See also* Ratings)
Differential survey treatments (DST),
149–150

Education, 61–64, 70, 125–126, 163–164
Employment, 64–66, 125–126, 163–164

Family, Hispanic, 124–131, 165
  bonds among members of, 126, 130
  and Catholic religion, 127
  children in, 125, 127, 131
  elders in, 127, 131
  imparting of social values, 127
  sex roles in, 130–131
  use of Spanish language, 89–90, 94,
    124–127
Federal Communications Commission
  (FCC), 143
Florida, 52, 55, 57–59
Focus groups, 123

Gallup Organization survey, *Listening and
  Viewing Habits of Hispanic Americans*,
  21–22, 41–42
General-market campaign (*see* Advertising
  campaign, general-market)
Generic Spanish, national versus regional
  approach to, 133–136
Gross rating points (GRPs), 153–154

History of Hispanic groups, 73–84
  in American society, 82–84
  (*See also* Cuba; Mexico; Puerto Rico)
Holidays, Hispanic, importance of, in
  public relations, 136–137

Illegal aliens (*see* Undocumented aliens)
Immigration to the United States,
  49–50, 59, 73–74, 83, 125, 164–165
  Cuban, 81–83
  Immigration and Naturalization Service,
    77–78
  Mexican, 76–78, 83
  Puerto Rican, 79–80, 83
Income, 6, 85
  by geographic region, 60–61
    table, 61
  of Hispanics versus U.S. total population,
    59–60, 70
  Los Angeles, 90
  Miami, 94
  New York, 89
  San Antonio, 94

Income (*Cont.*):
  by Spanish origin, 59–60
    table, 60

Jingles, 132
  (*See also* Commercials, use of music in)

KBSC-TV, Los Angeles, 35, 43, 143–144
KDTV, San Francisco, 35, 44
KEON-TV, Houston, 45, 143–144
KFTV, San Francisco, 35, 43
KLOC-TV, Sacramento-Stockton, 35, 44
KMEX-TV, Los Angeles, 35, 44
KORO-TV, Corpus Christi, 35, 45
KTVW-TV, Phoenix, 35, 43
KWEX-TV, San Antonio, 35, 45

Language use:
  English, 11, 125–126, 134, 165
    effect on media choices, 5–7, 11
    spoken at home, 89, 90, 94
  Spanish, 11, 69, 73–74, 82–84, 117,
    124–128, 165
    differences in style, 124, 133–135, 139
    effect on media choices, 5–7, 11, 18,
      23
    in public schools, 83, 125
    spoken at home, 89–90, 94, 124–126
    ties to country of origin, 124
Los Angeles, 52, 71, 141, 149
  Hispanic population (ADI), 89–92
    income, 90
    makeup, 89
    percent of U.S. total, 89
    product consumption indices, 90–92
    Spanish language use, 89–90
  as a test market, 115
Lotus Spanish Network, 145–146

Magazines:
  English, 3–5, 10–11, 166
  Spanish, 6, 9–12, 166
    advertising in, 12–13
    De Armas publications, 9–10, 147
    distribution of, 9–11
    editorial content of, 5, 9–12
    listings of, 13–15
    pass-along readership, 9–10
    (*See also* Media plan; Print)

Marketing information:
  availability of, 105
  Scott Paper Company case history,
    155–158
  (*See also* Consumer behavior;
    Demographics; Test market)
Media:
  English, 3–5, 7
    (*See also* Print, English; Radio,
      English; Television, English)
  Spanish, 5–7, 141–142
    (*See also* Magazines, Spanish;
      Newspapers, Spanish; Radio,
      Spanish; Television, Spanish)
Media content (*see* Magazines; Media;
    Newspapers; Radio; Television)
Media plan, 141–154, 166–167
  outdoor advertising, 141–142, 147
  print, 141–142, 146–147
  radio, 141–142, 144–146, 152
  Scott Paper Company case history,
    158–159
  television, 141–144
  transit advertising, 141–142, 147
  (*See also* Ratings; Reach and frequency)
Media segmentation, 3–5
  (*See also* Audience; National versus
    regional approach)
Median family income (*see* Income)
Mexicans in the United States, 83, 138–139
  advertising for, 134–135
  border markets, 68–69, 142
  education of, 62–64
  employment of, 64–66
  geographic concentration of, 52, 61
  household size of, 59
  immigration to the United States, 76–78,
    83
  income of, 59–61
  listening habits of, 18, 21
  metropolitan residence of, 66–67
  population size of, 52, 70
Mexico, 74–78
  American settlements in, 75
  braceros, 77
  independence of, 75
  migrant workers in, 76–78
  television in, 36–37, 142
  trade with the United States, 75
Miami, 52, 54, 71, 149
  Cuban exiles in, 81–82, 94
  Hispanic population (ADI), 94–97
    income, 94

Miami, Hispanic population
    (ADI) (*Cont.*):
  makeup, 94
  percent of U.S. total, 94
  product consumption indices, 95–97
  Spanish language use, 94
Migration (*see* Immigration to the United
    States; Undocumented aliens)
Music, 129, 135
  (*See also* Commercials)

National product usage (*see* Consumer
    behavior, Hispanic, national product
    usage)
National versus regional approach,
    133–136
Network, Spanish television (*see* SIN–
    National Spanish Television Network)
Neutral Spanish (*see* Generic Spanish)
Nevada, 75, 83
New Mexico, 55, 57–59, 74, 76, 83
New York City, 52, 54, 56, 70–71,
    137–139, 141, 144–145
  Hispanic population (ADI), 87–89
    income, 89
    makeup, 89
    percent of U.S. total, 89
    product consumption indices, 87–89
    Spanish language use, 89
  use of diaries in, 149
New York State, 55, 57–59
News, Spanish:
  in magazines, 5, 10, 12
  in newspapers, 11–12
  in radio, 6, 17–19
  in television, 6, 36, 40
Newspapers:
  English, 3–4, 9
  Spanish, 11–13, 146
    advertising rates of, 12
    editorial content of, 11–12
    listings of, 15–16
    weeklies, 12
Newsweek, 49
Nielsen, A. C., Co., 115, 147–153, 167
Novelas:
  in radio, 18
  in television, 37–39

Outdoor advertising, 141–142, 147
  (*See also* Media plan)

Personal placement and retrieval (PPR)
  technique, 149
Population (*see* Demographics)
Print:
  English, 3–4, 9, 131, 166
  Spanish, 9–16, 166
    as an advertising medium, 9–10,
      12–13, 141–142, 146–147
    (*See also* Magazines, Spanish;
      Newspapers, Spanish)
Product, 129, 136–138
  (*See also* Brand; Consumer behavior;
    Test market)
Product consumption indices (*see*
  Consumer behavior)
Product consumption levels,
  105–106
Product distribution, 137–138
Product quality, 129
Production, television (*see* Television,
  Spanish)
Public relations, 136–137
Puerto Ricans in the United States, 5, 52,
  79–80, 83, 139
  advertising for, 134–135
  education of, 61–64
  employment of, 64–66
  geographic concentration of, 52, 61,
    70–71
  immigration to the United States, 79–80,
    83
  income of, 59–61
  listening habits of, 21
  metropolitan residence of, 67
  population size of, 52, 70
Puerto Rico, 50–51, 78–80
  American influence in, 78–79
  Commonwealth status of, 79
  Spanish-American War, 78
  trade with the United States,
    78–79

Radio:
  English, 3–4, 7, 19–23, 131
  Spanish, 17–33, 36, 42, 152
    advertising, 22–23, 135–136, 141–142,
      144–146
    Arbitron Company reports, 19–22
    audience, 6–7, 18
      composition by age and sex, 21–22
      listening habits, 17, 19–23
    Caballero Spanish Media, 145–146

Radio, Spanish (*Cont.*):
  community involvement, 18–19,
    22–23, 42
    community calendars, 19
    public affairs programs, 18–19
  day-parts, 20–22
  Gallup Organization survey, 21–22
  Lotus Spanish Network, 145–146
  and media plan, 144–146
  music, 18, 135–136
  programming, 18–20, 165
  Southwest Spanish Broadcast Group,
    146
  station listings, 23–33
  (*See also* Ratings; Reach and
    frequency)
Ratings, 147–154
  Arbitron Company, 147–153, 167
  differential survey treatments (DST),
    149–150
  Nielsen, A. C., Co., 115, 147–153, 167
  personal placement and retrieval (PPR)
    technique, 149
  radio, 19–22
  television, 36, 39–42
  (*See also* Reach and frequency)
Reach and frequency, 23, 152–154
Research information:
  availability of, 105
  Scott Paper Company case history,
    155–158
  (*See also* Consumer behavior;
    Demographics; Test market)

Sales volume, Hispanic, 106
San Antonio, 135, 149
  Hispanic population (ADI), 92–94, 116
    income, 94
    makeup, 94
    percent of U.S. total, 94
  product consumption indices, 92–94
  Spanish language use, 94
  as a test market, 114–116
San Francisco, 18, 52, 71
Scott Paper Company:
  case history, 155–161
  spending in Hispanic market, graph, 161
Share of market (*see* Brand, product)
Share of voice, 107–108, 154, 167
SIN–National Spanish Television Network,
  35–36, 142–143
  border markets, 142

SIN–National Spanish Television
    Network (*Cont.*):
    cable systems, 35, 143, 166–167
    Census campaign, 38–39
    elections campaign, 39
    programming, 36, 38–39
        national news program, 36
    sales offices, 143
    translators, 35, 143, 166
Soap operas (see *Novelas*)
South Americans (*see* Central and South
    Americans in the United States)
Southwest Spanish Broadcast Group, 146
Spain, 73–75, 128
Spanish advertising (*see* Advertising,
    Hispanic)
Spanish broadcast media (*see* Media,
    Spanish)
Spanish print (*see* Print, Spanish)
Spanish Universal Network (SUN), 144
*Spanish USA—A Study of the Hispanic
    Market in the United States*, 52, 60,
    86, 124, 139
Specials, television, 38–39
Sports coverage, television, 7, 38, 40
Strategy Research Corporation, television
    audience measurement, 39–43, 148
SUN (Spanish Universal Network), 144

Target audience (*see* Audience)
Television:
    English, 4–7, 35–36, 131
    Spanish, 6–7, 35–45, 142–144, 166–167
        advertising, 42–43, 135–136, 141–142
        audience, 6–7
            composition by age and sex, 39–42
            Gallup Organization survey, 41–42
            shares, 35–36
        community involvement, 38–39, 42
        day-parts, 40–41
        independent stations, 35, 143–144
        and media plan, 141–144
        production, 6, 36, 166–167
        programming, 36–40, 144, 165–167
            comedies, 39
            news, 40
            novelas, 37–39
            specials, 38–39
            sports, 7, 38, 40
            variety shows, 7, 40

Television, Spanish (*Cont.*):
        ratings, 35–36, 39, 42
        SIN (*see* SIN–National Spanish
            Television Network)
        Spanish Universal Network (SUN), 144
        station listings, 43–45
        syndicated programs, 144, 166–167
        viewing habits, 35–42
        (*See also* Media plan; Ratings; Reach
            and frequency)
Test market, 107, 111–117
    case histories, 112–115
    selection of site, 115–116
Texas, 54–55, 57–59, 83
Time, 49
Transit advertising, 141–142, 147
    (*See also* Media plan)
Translators, 35, 143, 166
Twin cities (*see* Border markets)

Undocumented aliens, 49–50, 59, 69–70,
    76–78, 85, 106, 148, 164–165
    (*See also* Immigration to the United
        States)
Unduplicated audience, 152–154
    radio, 20–23
    television, 40–42
U.S. Bureau of the Census, 49–50, 55–56
    television public service campaign,
        38–39
U.S.–Mexico border, 75–78
U.S.–Mexico border markets, 68–69, 142
    table, 69
Usage incidences (*see* Consumer behavior;
    Product)

Variety shows, television, 7, 40
Venezuela, 50

WCIU-TV, Chicago, 35, 44
WLTV, Miami, 35, 37, 44
WNJU-TV, New York, 35, 37, 44, 143–144
WXTV, New York, 35, 37, 44

Yankelovich, Skelly & White, Inc. (see
    *Spanish USA—A Study of the Hispanic
    Market in the United States*)